200

Creative Crafts

for You & Your Home

SELLERS

PUBLISHING

Published by Sellers Publishing, Inc.
81 West Commercial Street
Portland, Maine 04101
For ordering information:
(800) 625-3386 toll free
(207) 772-6814 FAX
Visit our Web site: www.rsvp.com • E-mail: rsp@rsvp.com

President & Publisher: Ronnie Sellers
Publishing Director: Robin Haywood
Managing Editor: Mary Baldwin
Senior Editor: Megan Hiller
Assistant Production Editor: Charlotte Smith
Design: Heather Zschock
Photography: Sophie Boussahba, Claire Curt, Alain Montaufier, Isabelle Schaff
Translation: Roland Glasser

Thanks to Caroline Smith, Jocelyn Kahn, and Sally Smith of Caravan Beads, Inc., Portland, Maine; Marie Peck of Portland Fiber Gallery and Weaving Studio, Portland, Maine; and craft designers Amandine Dardenne, Katia Feder, Caroline Gibert, Françoise Hamon, Vanessa Pellerin, Marie-Pierre Schneegans, Charlotte Vannier, and Cyrielle Weimann.

ISBN 13: 978-1-56906-982-0
ISBN 10: 1-56906-982-4
LOC: 2007903309

Printed in India

10 9 8 7 6 5 4 3 2 1

200
Creative Crafts
for You & Your Home

Edited by Megan Hiller

Contents

Introduction

From simple and practical to wondrous and whimsical, this book offers ideas for a complete range of personal and gift projects. Divided into two parts — "crafts for you" and "crafts for your home," this book is further organized by type of project. Each section includes a wide range of crafting techniques including needle felting, sewing, crocheting, beading, painting, boondoggling, collage, and paper craft to help you create everything from personal fashion accessories to unique jewelry and one-of-a-kind decorations and creative ideas for your home or for gifts.

Learn to form designs in resin for jewelry or household items. Craft chokers, necklaces, bracelets, and rings with fabric, wire, felt, beads, and buttons. Practice charming napkin-folding techniques. Embellish and repurpose clothing, bags, furniture, and household goods using paper, wood, beads, buttons, wire, felt, and fabric, and by recycling other funky materials you have around your house.

This book will teach you to take everyday crafting items and use them in a fresh way. It may also introduce you to a whole range of new crafting items and ways to incorporate them into your projects. You will find most project materials in your local craft or specialty store (such as beading or fiber specialty shops). The Internet provides a vast marketplace for those items not easily found in your home or in local outlets.

The book's final sections include clearly illustrated techniques for those who are trying something new, as well as all the necessary patterns for the projects. The organized index will help you locate just what you're looking for.

PART ONE

Crafts for You

My New Bag

YOU WILL NEED:

- a handbag with wooden handles
- white wool fabric (to replace handbag's existing fabric)
- scissors
- plum-colored cotton thread
- white cotton thread
- a needle
- mother-of-pearl and shell buttons
- seed beads
- tube beads
- glass beads
- sewing machine
- hemp twine
- an upholstery needle
- 34 inches of plum-colored velvet ribbon (1 inch wide)

1. Remove the fabric from your bag and use the shape as a pattern to cut out a piece from the white wool fabric. Use the plum-colored cotton thread and the needle to sew the buttons onto the fabric in little flower patterns (*see photo*). Then take the seed beads, the tube beads, and the glass beads, and use the same needle and thread to sew star and flower motifs onto the fabric. Make a firm knot at the beginning and end of each little group of beads — that way if a thread breaks you will lose only some of the beads, not all of them. **2. Fold** the wool fabric in two, right sides together, and sew the two short sides together with the sewing machine. **3. Turn** the bag inside out and attach the upper edges of the bag to the wooden handles using the hemp twine and the upholstery needle. Pass the ribbon through the notches in the handles and sew the ends together with the plum-colored thread, making a 1-inch fold.

Seashell String Bag

YOU WILL NEED:

- a mini drill and drill bits
- seashells
- an orange cotton string bag
- a wool needle
- orange-colored beading thread
- beads
- pink shot taffeta
- seamstress's chalk
- pins
- scissors
- sewing machine
- a slender needle
- thread to match the taffeta
- thread that matches the taffeta

1. Use the mini drill to make holes in the center of the top of each shell. Sew the shells to the string bag using the wool needle and the orange beading thread. Use the same needle and thread to sew a string of beads and shells onto the side of the bag. **2. Place** the bag down flat on a piece of taffeta folded in two and trace its shape (except for the handles) using the seamstress's chalk, then pin the two parts of the taffeta together. Cut out using the scissors, taking care to leave an extra ⅓ inch, then overcast the fabric with the sewing machine to prevent fraying. With a slender needle and thread the color of the taffeta, use straight stitching to attach the taffeta lining to the bag, following the chalk line — make sure that you do not sew up the opening of the bag. Turn the taffeta lining inside out and slip it into the bag. Make a second line of stitches one-third of the way up from the first to secure the lining to the bag and to prevent the seam from showing.

Glasses Case

YOU WILL NEED:

- thick felt: dark green, mottled yellow
- scissors
- a needle
- matching green thread
- a medium paintbrush
- fabric glue

1. Trace out pattern A (*see p. 302*) at 200% on the green felt and cut it out. **2. Fold** it in two along the dotted line. Bourdon stitch it closed along the three straight sides. **3. Trace** out patterns B and C (*see p. 302*) on the yellow felt and cut them out. **4. Glue** piece B onto the case (well centered as shown in photograph) using the paintbrush to spread the glue evenly. **5. Glue** piece C onto the flap.

Forest Finds Bags

YOU WILL NEED:

- raw wood round slices (sliced at a slight angle) (¾ inch to 1¼ inches)
- a mini drill and drill bits
- acrylic paint (in 3 different colors)
- a small paintbrush
- oak leaf motif stamp
- white ink pad
- a felted wool bag with handle
- a small felted wool purse (approximately 4 x 6 inches)
- green thread
- a needle
- mother-of-pearl buttons
- beads
- little plastic flowers

1. Use the mini drill to make two holes in each wood slice, centering them in such a way that you create buttons. **2. Paint** the outside edge of some of the wood slices with acrylic paint and stamp an oak leaf motif on the rest, using the stamp. Allow to dry. **3. Sew** the wood slices onto the bag and the purse (randomly spaced) using the green thread and then sew mother-of-pearl buttons, beads, or little plastic flowers into some of the wood slice centers.

Little Flat Bag

YOU WILL NEED:

- strong green striped cotton fabric (35 x 12 inches)
- blue-green lining fabric (35 x 12 inches, 6 x 5 inches for the inside pocket)
- 2 pieces of black Velcro (8 inches long)
- sewing machine
- thread to match fabric; thread to match lace
- iron
- pins
- 12 inches of teal-blue grosgrain ribbon (1 inch wide)
- 12 inches of light pink lace (1 inch wide)
- 24 inches of teal-blue sewn sequin ribbon
- 2 buttons of matching color but different sizes
- cotton strap (1 yard long)

1. **Overcast** all of the pieces of fabric on a sewing machine to prevent fraying. 2. **Press** pleat points on the long strips of fabric and lining: the first, 12 inches from the end of the piece of fabric (flap pleat), and the second, 24 inches from the end of the piece of fabric (bag bottom pleat). 3. **Make** a hem ⅓ of an inch in width along one of the long sides of the bag. Press the hems along the other three sides with an iron. Pin to the central part of the lining and stitch on three sides. 4. **Pin** the gripping part of the Velcro strip to the upper part of the lining. Machine stitch. 5. **Pin** the soft part of the Velcro strip to the lower part of the cotton fabric, taking care to place it accurately in relation to the strip sewn on the lining. Machine stitch. 6. **Place** the grosgrain ribbon on the upper part of the fabric (the front of the bag). Attach it with matching thread in discreet hand stitches along the edges. Then position the pink lace perpendicular to it. Attach it with matching thread in discreet hand stitches. Attach the sequin ribbon along each edge of the lace strip. Lastly, attach the buttons, placing the larger one beneath the smaller one. 7. **Pin** the strap by placing it on the central part of the fabric (the inside of the bag). Place the ends in the upper corners by folding them back on themselves to a length of 3 inches. Machine stitch them, going over the grosgrain ribbon. 8. **Sew** the two lower parts of the fabric right sides together, ⅓ inch from the edge, stopping ⅓ inch from the upper edge. 9. **Sew** the upper part of the lining and the fabric, right sides together, ⅓ inch from the edge. Turn over this flap and pin the two remaining edges, leaving ⅓-inch fold. Attach the flap with discreet hand stitches.

A Purse for Everything

YOU WILL NEED:

- purple wool felt fabric
- scissors
- sewing machine
- purple thread
- pink carded wool roving and/or top
- purple carded wool roving and/or top
- a foam cushion (a piece of dense foam rubber, 1½ to 2 inches thick)
- a felting needle
- a snap
- fabric glue
- a needle

1. **Trace** out the purse pattern (*see p. 303*) on the felt. Cut out the purse ¼ of an inch from the edge and then cut out the flap along the seam. 2. **Use** the sewing machine to sew a tight overcast stitch (like something you would use for a monogram) along the edge of the flap (see photo). 3. **Fold** the purse in half and stitch the edges together. Turn the purse inside out so the stitching is inside. 4. **To needle-felt** the flower, take a little of the pink wool and shape it with your fingers. Place it on the foam and poke it into the shape of one petal. Take another little piece of pink wool, shape another petal, and poke it into the base of the first petal. Repeat needle-felting process until you have made a flower with five petals. Take a little of the purple wool, shape it with your fingers, place it in the center of the flower, and poke it into place (making sure that the foam is underneath). 5. **Sew** the snap inside the flap. Glue the flower onto the outside of the flap.

Orchard Basket

YOU WILL NEED:

- paper napkins with fig motifs
- scissors
- a mauve plastic tote basket
- adhesive varnish
- a flat paintbrush

1. Carefully cut the fig designs from the paper napkins and remove all but the top printed layer. **2. Cover** part of the lower half of the basket with adhesive varnish. Place one strip of paper fig designs on the lower part of the basket. Cover them with adhesive varnish. **3. Then place** another strip until you have gone all the way around the bottom half of the basket. Cover the whole basket with a coat of adhesive varnish so as to avoid differences in shininess. Leave it to dry. **4. Cover** the whole surface with another coat of adhesive varnish for evenness.

Flower Carryall

YOU WILL NEED:

- sewing machine
- dark green cotton (13 x 17 inches and 28 x 4 inches)
- dark green thread
- pins
- seamstress's chalk
- iron
- yellow thread

- a needle
- orange flower-print cotton fabric (approx. 30 x 5 inches)
- orange lining (approx. 20 x 4 inches)
- yellow fabric (16 x 2 inches)
- yellow, red, and orange opaque seed beads
- orange lining (approx. 20 x 4 inches)

To make the bag: 1. With a sewing machine, overcast each piece of dark green fabric to prevent fraying. **2. Pin** and then stitch a 1½-inch hem along one of the widths of each large rectangle. **3. Pin** the two large rectangles right sides together and trace the seams ⅓ of an inch from the edges without a hem, using seamstress's chalk. Mark out the curves of the lower corners ½ inch from the edge, using an upside-down bowl. Cut along the curves, ½ inch from the drawn line. Overcast. Machine stitch, following the drawn line. Turn inside out and press with an iron. **4. Fold** the two strips of green fabric in half lengthways. Pin, then stitch, them together ⅓ inch from the edge. **5. Turn** inside out, then press with a hot iron, centering the seam. Use a simple top stitch to create decorative curves in yellow thread on the handles, using the sewing machine. **6. Pin** the handles onto the bag, then attach them with tight front stitches, using the sewing machine. **7. Sew** the two edges of the handles together by hand across a centered area of 7½ inches, using tack stitches. Turn the bag inside out.

To make the flower: 8. Photocopy the petal pattern (*see p. 303*) in three different sizes (two at approx. 4 x 4 inches and one at 2 x 2 inches). **9. Using** the patterns, cut six large petals from the flower-print cotton fabric, five medium petals from the orange lining, and three small ones from the yellow fabric. **10. Attach** the large petals to the bag one by one, slipping one bead onto each stitch. Repeat for the other petals. **11. Cut** out one disk from the yellow fabric 2 inches in diameter. Overcast it. Sew a few beads into its center, then pass a gathering stitch along its edge, and pull tight. **12. Sew** this little ball of fabric into the heart of the flower.

Felt Bag

YOU WILL NEED:

- felt: beige for the bag, mottled brown for the sides, and smaller pieces of dark brown, blue, and white for accents
- scissors
- beige thread and sewing machine (optional)
- fabric glue

1. Enlarge the pattern (*see p. 307*) 300% (twice at 150%) and print out two copies. Trace or pin the patterns to the beige felt and cut them out. Cut out the rectangle in the middle to form the handles. **2. Cut** a strip measuring 1½ wide x approximately 26 inches long from the mottled brown felt. **3. Use** this long strip of felt to form the sides and bottom of the bag by machine stitching or gluing it to the two pieces of beige felt. **4. Cut** a 2-inch square from the white felt. Cut two 1¼-inch squares from the dark brown felt. Cut two 1-inch squares from the blue felt. Cut three ¾-inch squares from the beige felt. Place these felt squares as shown in the photo and glue them. Leave to dry.

Little Beaded Pouch

YOU WILL NEED:

- mottled light-green felt
- scissors
- green thread
- a needle

- green glass beads
- green seed beads
- a snap

1. Enlarge the pattern (*see p. 304*) on a photocopier to desired size and print out. Pin the pattern to the light-green felt. Cut the pouch part ⅓ of an inch from the edge and cut out the flap along the dotted line. **2. Fold** the pouch in two, right sides together, sew it, and then turn it right side out. **3. Sew** little glass beads around the edge and in the middle of the flap. **4. Sew** a few seed beads here and there on the front of the pouch. **5. Sew** on the press stud fastener.

Spring Fling Bag

YOU WILL NEED:

- ½ yard green cotton (plain or patterned) cut in 2 squares each measuring 8⅔ inches
- ½ yard plain pink cotton cut in 2 squares each measuring 8⅔ inches
- needle and thread for overcasting fabric edges
- pink thread
- ½ yard fuchsia-pink lining material
- turquoise-colored corded cotton thread
- pink-colored corded cotton thread
- 13 rhinestones in pink, green, and orange
- iron
- fabric glue
- 24 inches turquoise grosgrain ribbon (¾ inch wide)

1. **Overcast** stitch the pieces of cotton fabric to prevent fraying (except for the fuchsia-pink lining material). 2. **Photocopy** the petal and butterfly-wing patterns at 100% (see p. 309). Cut out 16 petals and two butterfly wings from the fuchsia-pink lining material. Blanket stitch the edge of eight petals, using the turquoise or pink thread. 3. **Create** an eight-petal flower on the square of green fabric that will form the front of the bag. Four of the petals should be edged ones. Fix the petals to the bag using herringbone stitches and glue three rhinestones in the center, which will form the heart of the flower. Slightly lift the petals and glue one rhinestone at the tip of each. 4. **Edge** the butterfly wings with a running stitch in turquoise thread. Pin the two wings together and make the butterfly's body with a line of herringbone stitches. Use a stem stitch to embroider short antennae. Glue one rhinestone for the eye. 5. **Sew** the squares of green fabric right sides together a ¼ of an inch from the edge. Turn over and press. Repeat the steps using the pink fabric. Slip the pink bag into the green bag. 6. **Cut** the turquoise ribbon in two. Slip the two pieces between the bags and pin them in place. Pin the bag and its lining together, including ¼-inch hem fold for each one. Sew using a discreet hem stitch.

Summer Bag

YOU WILL NEED:

- seamstress's chalk
- green upholstery fabric with large printed pattern (22 x 16 inches)
- orange lining fabric (22 x 16 inches)
- scissors
- sewing machine
- pins
- iron

- 31 inches of orange cotton webbing (2 inches wide)
- orange sewing thread
- 31 inches of flexible plastic tubing (⅓ inch in diameter) such as one finds in a home improvement store
- a utility knife and cutting mat

1. Use seamstress's chalk to mark out the curves of the lower edges of the four fabric rectangles, using a small bowl turned upside down. Cut out, then overcast the four sides to prevent fraying. **2. Pin** right sides together, the two rectangles of fabric on three sides, leaving the top open, then sew them together at ⅓ of an inch from the edge. Stop the seam 10 inches from the top edge on the two sides. Repeat the operation with the rectangles of lining fabric, right sides together. **3. Turn** the two bags inside out and slip the bag made of upholstery fabric inside that made of lining fabric. Pin the four short sides right sides together and stitch with the sewing machine. Turn inside out and iron. **4. Cut** the strip of cotton webbing in two. Fold each piece in two lengthways and stitch together along the edge. Cut the plastic tubing with the utility knife and slip a piece into each orange handle. **5. Finish** the top of the bag: fold and press with an iron the upholstery and lining fabrics and add a small hem. Pin the stitch close to the edge. Repeat this operation on the other side. **6. Slip** the handles into the conduits you just made and sew their ends together by hand.

My Makeup Bag

YOU WILL NEED:

- scissors
- thick orange felt
- a small felted wool pouch with zipper closure
- thread
- a needle
- a mother-of-pearl button (30 mm or 1 inch in diameter)
- gilded metal wire
- wire cutters
- round-nose pliers
- a few small crystal beads (various shapes and colors)
- 2 small gilded beads
- 1 small gilded jump ring
- contact glue
- a blue multifaceted bead (12 mm in diameter)
- a flat-headed nail
- a small jump ring

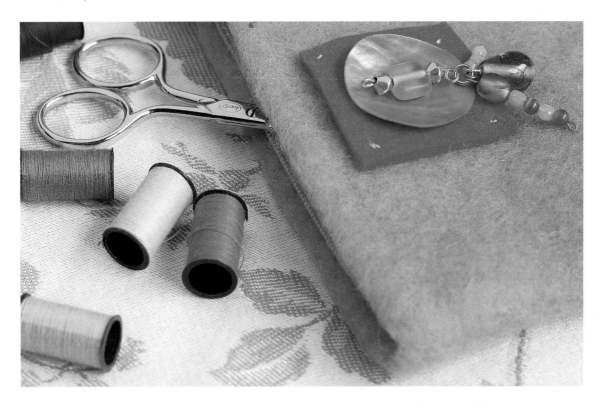

1. Cut out a 2-inch square of orange felt. Fix it to the pouch with a single stitch in each corner. Sew the button onto it. **2. Take** three short lengths of metal wire and use the round-nose pliers to make a small closing loop in one end of each. String a few small crystal beads onto the wires. Use the round-nose pliers to attach the three beaded wires to a gilded jump ring. Cut another small length of wire and attach a gilded bead, a crystal bead (with a flat side), and another gilded bead. Make small loops at both ends and attach to the gilded jump ring. Add a spot of contact glue to a flat side of the middle bead on this last wire and use it to secure the entire beaded piece to the button. **3. Place** the large multifaceted bead on the flat-headed nail. Make a loop with the pliers and link it to the zipper using a small jump ring.

Freshly Hatched Bag

YOU WILL NEED:

- a utility knife
- a plastic egg box (for a dozen eggs)
- cream-colored webbing strap (2 inches wide)
- cream-colored plastic handles
- white or transparent glue
- scissors
- light-colored heat-seal fabric
- flower-print fabric
- iron
- sewing machine
- thread
- cream-colored bias tape
- clothespins (or similar clips)

1. Use the utility knife to cut off the original handles of the egg box (found in camping section of stores). Carefully cut two slits the same width as the webbing strap where the plastic handles were. **2. Pass** a piece of webbing strap through each of the slits, from the inside to the outside; place a plastic handle over each one; then pass the webbing straps back through the slits to the inside. Secure the handles by gluing the two ends of each webbing strap onto the plastic box. **3. To make** the interior lining, copy the pattern on page 308, taking care to adapt it to the size and shape of the box you are using. Cut the heat-seal fabric according to your completed pattern. Heat-seal the flower-print fabric on top of it using an iron (an old one if possible). Mark the pleats well. **4. Sew** a small piece of bias tape along the top of each gusset. **5. Glue** the fabric inside the box. Use clothespins to hold the fabric securely to the box until the glue has dried fully.

Bag of Secrets

YOU WILL NEED:

- black and white striped cotton fabric (8¾ x 17¾ inches)
- 1 yard and 13 inches of pale-pink satin ribbon (2 inches wide)
- sewing machine
- iron
- black thread
- a needle
- a safety pin

1. **Overcast** the four sides of the piece of fabric with a sewing machine. 2. **Make** a 5-inch wide turnup on one of the ends rights sides together, pin it then press it with a hot iron. 3. **Use** the iron to mark a ¹/₃-inch hem fold on the edge of the turnup. 4. **Make** two parallel seams along the length, spaced 1½ inches apart. 5. **To close** the bottom of the bag, make a seam ⅓ inch from the edges, right sides together, without going past the first horizontal seam. 6. **Turn** the bag inside out and iron it. Close the ruffle using hand-stitched petit points. 7. **Use** the safety pin to slide the ribbon through the ruffle, pull it tight, and knot it.

Winter Bag

YOU WILL NEED:

- 2 pieces of green motif-printed needle cord fabric (one 17⅔ x 13⅓ inches, the other 19⅔ x 6¾ inches)
- green thread
- pins
- sewing machine
- iron
- 4 inches of Velcro (1¼ inches wide)
- matching lining (one 17⅔ x 13⅓ inches, the other 6 x 4¾ inches)

- 1 yard plus 15 inches of flesh-pink lace (2 inches wide)
- a needle
- pink thread
- 23½ inches of brown satin ribbon (⅓ inch wide)
- 1 yard plus 3 inches of olive-green satin ribbon (⅓ inch wide)
- a medium-size bead

To make the bag: 1. Overcast stitch all of the pieces of needle cord fabric to prevent fraying. **2. With** right sides together, pin the two rectangles of the needle cord and stitch them ⅓ of an inch from the edge, leaving one of the smaller sides open. **3. To make** the flat bottom of the bag (the bag is still inside out), lay the side seam over the bottom seam in each sewn corner. Pin together. Make a mark at 2 inches from the corner on each side, then trace a line between these points. Stitch along this line and cut off the excess at ⅓ of an inch from the seam. Overcast this new raw edge. Repeat on the other side. Turn the bag inside out and iron, ensuring that you make the corners really flat. **4. Cut** the Velcro strip in two. Use the sewing machine to stitch the four pieces (two velvety pieces and two with the little hooks) onto what will become the top edge of the lining, at 2 inches from the edge. **5. Pin** a hem on the smaller piece of lining and mark it with a hot iron. Stitch the long side only, which will form the opening of the pocket. **6. Pin** the pocket onto one of the pieces of lining, underneath the Velcro. Stitch it on three sides. **7. Pin** the two rectangles of lining right sides together and stitch them together ⅓ of an inch from the edge, leaving the side with the Velcro open. Make the flat bottom according to the same method as in step 3 above. **8. To make** the strap, fold the strip of needle cord fabric in two lengthways. Pin together then stitch at ⅓ of an inch from the edge. Turn the lining inside out then press with a hot iron, taking care to center the seam. Center each end of the strap on a side seam of the bag, and pin it in place. **9. Slip** the lining into the bag. Pin the bag and lining together along the opening, making a ⅓-inch-wide turnup for each one. Stitch near to the edge. **10. Sew** on the lace at the top and bottom by hand, using an invisible needlepoint stitch. **To make the flower: 11. Make** a lot of little loops with the brown and green satin ribbon — mixing them up. Let two 10-inch lengths of brown ribbon hang down and bias-cut their ends. **12. Pin** the loops as you go, then hand-stitch a bead to the center of the flower. **13. Hand-stitch** the flower to the base of the strap.

Spring Flower Bag

YOU WILL NEED:

- 2 rectangles of linen measuring 13¾ x 11¾ inches
- 2 rectangles of beige-colored thin cotton fabric measuring 13¾ x 11¾ inches
- sewing machine
- thread: white, green, and beige
- iron
- pins
- bright pink bias tape
- a tape measure
- a sheet of laminated flowers
- scissors

1. **Enlarge** the pattern (approximately 220%) on page 310 and trace it out on the two rectangles of cotton fabric and on the two rectangles of linen. Pin the two pieces of cotton right sides together and do the same for the two pieces of linen. Use the sewing machine to stitch the two pieces of cotton together, using a straight stitch 2 inches from the edge — sew the bottom and sides of the bag, but leave the top open. Do the same with the two pieces of linen, then turn the bag inside out, and press with an iron. Slip the cotton bag (not turned inside out) into the linen one and adjust the two openings so that the edges line up. Pin the bias tape over the top edges of the bag (*see A on p.310*) and stitch with the sewing machine. Cut off the extra bias at the ends of these edges. Cut a 37-inch length of bias and place it over the edges (B) and (C), leaving an excess to form the handles above edge (A). Front stitch using the sewing machine along the whole length of the bias folded in two. 2. **Cut** out nine disks from the sheet of laminated flowers, place them on the front of the bag, and sew to the bag with two tack stitches on the left and right of each disk.

Black Button Bag

YOU WILL NEED:

- a bag (made of plastic, preferably with a gusset)
- cross-section paper
- scissors
- pencil
- a tagging gun
- tagging gun fasteners (1-inch long)
- black buttons (number needed depends on the size of your bag and the size of the buttons)

1. Cut the paper to the size of the bag. Draw a grid of ⅔-inch squares with a pencil. Keep the paper pressed down onto the bag and make holes with the tagging gun at each grid intersection — make sure that you perforate both the paper and the bag. Make all of the holes into which you will insert the plastic fasteners **2. Place** a set of fasteners into the tagging gun. Take a button and stick the gun's needle into the buttonhole. Press the needle into the bag on the grid intersection defined by the sheet of paper. Press the trigger of the tagging gun to punch the end of the tag through the side of the bag. Release the trigger and withdraw the needle. Proceed in this way for the rest of the buttons. **Tip:** Tagging guns and fasteners may be found in shops stocking items for the retail sector (shelving accessories, labels, packaging, etc.).

Purse

YOU WILL NEED:

- seamstress's chalk
- 2 pieces of orange flower-print linen (15¾ x 13 inches)
- 2 pieces of plum-colored lining fabric (13¾ x 13 inches)
- scissors
- a needle
- plum-colored sewing thread
- pins
- sewing machine
- iron
- 1 yard plus 3 inches of orange-colored grosgrain ribbon
- a safety pin

1. Use seamstress's chalk to mark curved corners on the bottom sides of the four rectangles of fabric with the aid of an upturned pie plate. Cut out the curved corners and overcast stitch them to prevent fraying. **2. Pin**, then sew, the two rectangles of linen right sides together at ⅓ of an inch from the edge. Halt the seam at 2¾ inches from the end of one of the two sides. Turn inside out and press with an iron. Repeat the operation with the rectangles of lining fabric, but without turning the resulting bag inside out. **3. Slip** the lining into the linen bag. Pin, then stitch, a hem ⅓ of an inch wide along that part of the side seam that is unsewn. **4. Finish** the top of the bag: Fold the linen back on itself to a width of ⅓ of an inch, then again to a width of 1¼ inches to form the tunnel that will carry the ribbon. Stitch along the fold. **5. Hand-sew** little hems at the ends of the ribbon. Slip the ribbon through the tunnel with the aid of a safety pin.

Frilly Bracelet

YOU WILL NEED:

- 4 feet of green and pink moiré organza ribbon
- scissors
- thread
- a needle
- 14 green and pink opaline multi-facetted beads (4 mm diameter)
- 6 dark red pearly satin beads (4 mm diameter)
- 7 green pearly cat's eye beads (4 mm diameter)
- 2 fold-over ends
- flat-nose pliers
- silvered spring ring clasp

1. **Cut** out a piece of ribbon to fit around your wrist. 2. **Make** nine "flowers" — for each of them cut out approximately 4 inches of ribbon; sew these ribbons lengthways, then scrumple them up to make flower shapes. 3. **Once** you have made the nine "flowers," sew them onto the bracelet one by one, sewing 3 different beads into the center of each one as you do so. 4. **Once** you have sewn the flowers onto the ribbon, take the scissors and carefully trim the edges of the flowers to give them a rougher look. The edges will fray quite naturally. 5. **Finish** by attaching a fold-over end to each end of the bracelet and close with the pliers. Attach to the clasp.

Cherub Brooch

YOU WILL NEED:

- metal wire
- wire cutters
- round-nose pliers
- 3-4 fancy beads
- 7 multifaceted crystal beads (6 and 8 mm in diameter)
- 2 small pieces of frosted glass
- a bead cap
- a flat-headed nail
- a small metal cherub charm
- a leaf bead or charm
- a kilt pin with seven stationary loops
- 7 inches (approximately) of organza ribbon

1. **Take** a small piece of metal wire, make a small loop in one end using the round-nose pliers, string one bead onto it, then fix it in place with another loop. Mount each fancy or multifaceted bead individually onto a piece of metal wire in this way. (Leave one fancy bead without wire for use with the bead cap later.) 2. **Wind** metal wire around two pieces of glass, as if you were wrapping a present, and finish with a loop. 3. **String** the beads together, linking the loops, in sections of different lengths, aiming for a harmonious mix. End one of these sections with a bead cap enclosing a bead fixed on a flat-headed nail. Attach the cherub to the longest section. Attach the leaf bead to the end of one section. 4. **Attach** each completed section of beads to the loops of the kilt pin and knot one piece of ribbon to it.

Dancing Girl Brooch

YOU WILL NEED:

- thin metal wire
- wire cutters
- round-nose pliers
- 2 round frosted beads (8 mm in diameter)
- a round frosted bead (6 mm in diameter)
- 2 multifaceted crystal beads (8 mm in diameter)
- a green fancy bead
- 6 inches of coppered chain
- a round frosted bead (8 mm in diameter)
- a little gilded bead cap
- matte seed beads
- tube beads
- coppered jump rings (5 mm diameter)
- coppered kilt pin with 7 stationary loops

1. Take a short length of thin metal wire and use the round-nose pliers to make a loop in one end. String a bead onto it and close it in place with another loop. Use this procedure to string the 6 beads listed in the materials. **2. Cut** 6 pieces of chain of differing lengths and hook one bead setup onto each of them. Set them aside until you are ready to attach everything to the pin. **3. To make** the little girl: String one frosted bead, the cup bead, and one seed bead into the middle of 8 inches of thin metal wire. Using the seed bead as the end bead, thread the one end of the wire back through the cup bead and the frosted bead. Leave enough wire on each side to make two arms. String 3 or 4 tube beads followed by a seed bead on each arm wire. Again, use the seed bead as the end bead and rethread the remaining wire back through the last tube bead. Trim off any excess wire. **4. The dress** is a little triangle of woven seed beads. Fold 20 inches of wire in half. Begin the weave by stringing one bead into the center of the 20 inches. Cross the wires and add 2 beads to make the next row. Continue to cross the wires and add beads, increasing the number of beads on each line. Each row of beads will have wires through it in each direction. The last line should have 10 beads strung on it (*see p. 302*). **5. Making** the legs: Rethread the wires part way through the longest row of beads so that the wires are coming out the bottom in a centered spot. String a few tube beads onto each of these two lengths of wire. Rethread each length of wire through the second to last bead and then cut it off. **6. Link** the head and body together. Use the jump rings to mount the chains and the girl to the kilt pin.

Pea Pod Brooch

YOU WILL NEED:

- red-brown polymer clay
- a rolling pin
- gold leaf
- a utility knife
- contact glue
- a brooch pin

1. Roll a little of the clay between your fingers in order to soften it. Use the rolling pin to roll out a flat piece about ⅛ of an inch thick. **2. Carefully** place one sheet of gold leaf on this piece, then flatten it out across the whole surface using the rolling pin. **3. Turn** the piece over and repeat the gilding process. The gold leaf will crack apart as it is rolled into the clay. **4. Fold** the piece of clay in half and trace the shape of a pea pod using the point of the utility knife. Cut out the two sides of the pod and mold them together along the base. **5. Use** the rest of the gilded clay to form little balls of different sizes and place them inside the pod. Add a little more gilding to the balls if necessary. **6. Bake** the finished piece in a very low oven for about ten minutes (place it on a sheet of parchment paper). **7. Once** the piece has cooled, glue the brooch pin to one of its sides.

Velvet Choker

YOU WILL NEED:

- 28 inches of green velvet ribbon (½ inch wide)
- seamstress's chalk
- assorted transparent seed beads
- brightly colored sequins and stars

- 22 inches of pale pink satin ribbon (¼ inch wide)
- matching thread

1. Take the green velvet ribbon and measure out two turns of your neck, starting at the nape. Make a chalk mark on the parts of the ribbon that are in line with your chin. **2. Use** the seed beads to attach the stars and sequins to the ribbon, placing them in an attractive arrangement around the chalk marks. **3. Hand-stitch** a little hem at each end of the velvet ribbon. **4. Cut** the satin ribbon in two. Sew each end to the reverse of each end of the velvet ribbon, then use a star and a seed bead to mask the stitching on the outside. Bias cut the ends of the satin ribbons.

Mother-of-Pearl Choker

YOU WILL NEED:

- a silvered metal choker
- fine navy-blue metal wire (approximately 28 gauge)
- a tape measure
- wire cutters
- very fine beading wire (.012, 49-strand)
- crimp beads
- flat-nose pliers
- little translucent light-blue and navy-blue tube beads
- oval translucent glass beads
- mother-of-pearl beads in different sizes, shapes, and colors

1. Wrap the metal choker with the navy-blue wire to cover approximately ⅓ inch worth of the choker. Trim the wire at the end of the wrap so that the point end will not be against your skin. **2. Take** a length of the very fine beading wire, make a tight loop around the choker at the point where you stopped wrapping the metal wire, and use a crimp bead to crimp it in place. String several beads, a crimp bead, and a mother-of-pearl button onto this length of wire. Pull the wire through one of the buttonholes then double-back through the crimp bead, and crimp it closed. Pass another piece of wire through the second hole of the button and block it with a crimp bead. String several more beads onto the thread, then attach the thread to another button using a crimp bead. Continue in this way until you have reached a total length of around 6 inches. Use another crimp bead to attach the end of this string of beads and buttons to the metal choker. Make five such strings of beads and buttons and attach them all to the metal choker in an overlapping fashion. **3. Leave** about 1 inch between each attachment point. Wrap the bare choker between these points with the navy-blue wire as you did in the first step. Add final ⅓ inch of navy-blue wire to complete the piece.

Braided Bracelet

YOU WILL NEED:

- a premade threaded plait
- colorless varnish
- a paintbrush
- scissors
- a ruler
- double-sided sticky tape
- orange bias tape (½ inch wide)
- sewing machine
- orange thread
- flat-nose pliers
- 2 flat crimp-ends (1½ inches long)
- 2 oval rings
- a clasp

1. Place the thread plait on a sheet of paper and paint one side of it with the colorless varnish. Do not use too much varnish, otherwise it will soak through the plait. Leave the plait to dry on another clean sheet of paper. **2. Cut** off approximately 6 inches of plait according to the size of your wrist and the length of the clasp and rings you will be using to close the bracelet. Round off the corners using the scissors. **3. Place** double-sided sticky tape along the entire length of the bias tape, which will be about 15 inches (twice the length and twice the width). Apply the bias tape, starting in the middle of the plait. Progress carefully, removing the protective film little by little as you go. Straight stitch the bias along its entire inside edge. **4. Crimp** one flat crimp-end to each extremity of the bracelet. Add the oval rings and the clasp.

Sea Anemone Ring

YOU WILL NEED:

- fine nylon thread
- scissors
- 30 (approximate) white frosted drop beads (4 x 6 mm in size) drilled through at top and bottom
- 30 (approximate) matte brown seed beads
- a copper-plated metal ring finding mounted with a flat pierced open-work setting

For the alternative piece:

- fine nylon thread
- scissors
- 6 green drop beads (6 x 9 mm in size) drilled through at the top point
- a brass-plated metal ring finding mounted with a pierced open-work setting
- a rhinestone (8 mm in diameter)
- a gilded perforated claw setting for a rhinestone (8 mm in diameter)
- gem glue

1. **Using** approximately 1 yard of nylon thread, pass the thread successively through the base of one drop bead, one seed bead, then double back through the drop bead (*see p. 304*). 2. **Attach** each bead to the ring base by passing the thread through a perforation. 3. **Bring** the thread up through the next perforation and add another bead set. Continue in this way, ensuring that the beads are packed tightly together. Secure the final bead set by bringing the thread down through an opening in the setting and knotting it tightly. **Variant:** flower with green drop beads 1. **String** the six drop beads onto the nylon thread to form a six-petal flower. Pass the ends of the thread though the beads twice and bring them out at two opposite points. 2. **Attach** the flower securely to the ring base with the nylon thread, making several knots. 3. **Place** the rhinestone in the setting and close the claws. To attach the rhinestone setting to the ring, pass two lengths of nylon thread through the perforations of the settings, then under the ring. Secure the setting in place with several knots and a spot of glue.

Seed Necklace

YOU WILL NEED:

- crystal resin
- resin hardener
- a little plastic pot (e.g. film canister)
- a plastic pot
- transparent resin dye
- a plastic spoon or craft stick
- silicon chocolate molds
- dried seeds or beans
- beading wire (should match jump rings in thickness and color)
- wire cutters
- needle-nose pliers
- fancy beads
- a mini-drill and drill bits
- jump rings (large quantity)

1. **Use** the little plastic pot to measure out and pour two parts crystal resin and one part resin hardener into the larger plastic pot, then add a few drops of resin dye to the mixture. Mix with the plastic spoon, stirring slowly to prevent bubbles forming. Half fill the silicon molds with resin and leave them to dry for about 12 hours. 2. **Place** the seeds or beans on top of the half-hardened resin in the molds in such a way as to create patterns, then cover them with the same resin/hardener mixture as before. Leave the molds to dry for 24 hours so that they harden fully, then turn out the resin discs. 3. **Take** a small length of metal wire (1¼-inch long) and use the needle-nose pliers to form a loop at one end. String a fancy bead on the wire and fix it in place by making a second loop. Repeat this process to fix all your fancy beads on metal wire. 4. **Use** the mini-drill to pierce holes in the resin discs, as well as in several beans, and string all of these elements together using the jump rings, which you can then close with the needle-nose pliers.

Cozy Necklace

YOU WILL NEED:

- multicolored looped wool
- a crochet needle
- a tape measure
- scissors
- mother-of-pearl buttons of different sizes and colors
- nylon thread
- little crimp beads
- a crimp tube clasp
- flat-nose pliers

1. Take the wool and make slip stitches using the crochet needle (*see p. 296*), leaving approximately 10 inches of unstitched wool at the start. Crochet the wool to a length of approximately 12½ inches. Leave another 10 inches of unstitched wool and cut the wool from the ball. **2. Repeat** the procedure twice and plait together the three unstitched threads at each end. Attach the buttons to the wool necklace using a piece of nylon thread that you pass through each button, binding them tightly to the necklace by placing crimp beads on the back of the necklace. **3. Place** the buttons across the whole necklace in an irregular fashion, varying the colors and the shapes. Fold the plaited threads of wool in half at a distance of ⅓ of an inch from the start and place the crimp tube clasp around them. Use the flat-nose pliers to crimp the clasp shut and cut off any excess wool.

Even Cozier Necklace

YOU WILL NEED:

- several colored decorative buttons
- crocheted wool flowers
- silver-plated fine metal wire
- wire cutters
- red, pink, and mauve seed beads
- assorted colors of cotton thread
- a needle
- plum-colored velvet ribbon (¾ inch wide)
- scissors
- a tape measure
- a snap

1. Attach a button to the center of each of the wool flowers, using a small piece of silver-plated metal wire. Embroider the beads around the edges of the flowers, varying the colors with the assorted cotton thread. **2. Cut** a length of 15 inches from the plum-colored velvet ribbon and sew the flowers to it in a regularly spaced manner. **3. Turn up** a ½ inch wide edge at each end of the ribbon and sew it using tightly spaced small stitches. Attach the snap with a few stitches.

Baroque Earrings with Little Rhinestones

YOU WILL NEED:

- 2 copper-colored square filigree pierced open-work ring settings
- 6 small round copper charms
- 2 small copper cross-shaped pierced open-work ring settings
- 2 mauve rhinestones (8 mm in diameter)
- 2 mauve rhinestones (6 mm in diameter)
- 6 mauve rhinestones (4 mm in diameter)
- gem glue
- ultra-fine copper-plated metal wire
- wire cutters
- gray iridescent seed beads
- 10 copper-plated jump rings (3-4 mm diameter)
- round-nose pliers
- a pair of copper-plated earring hooks with clasps

1. **Glue** all of the rhinestones onto the various pierced open-work ring settings as in the picture. Leave to dry. 2. **Cut** off about 40 inches of ultrafine wire. Pass it through one of the holes on the edge of the pierced open-work ring settings and use the pliers to attach it in place as a beginning point. String one bead onto it until it rests on the edge of the pierced open-work ring setting. Pass the wire through the next hole and string another bead onto it. Continue to attach beads in this way all around the edge of the pierced open-work ring settings. Use the pliers to close off the wire on the reverse of the pierced open-work ring setting. 3. **Place** a few beads on the small pierced open-work ring settings in the same way. 4. **Now** use the jump rings to link the various elements composing the earring together. For each earring: three little charms linked to the base of the large pierced open-work ring setting, in turn linked to the smaller pierced open-work ring setting, which is then linked to the clasp on the hook.

Felt Heart Choker

YOU WILL NEED:

- white wool felt
- scissors
- light-green carded wool roving and/or top
- a foam cushion
- a felting needle
- Velcro
- fabric glue

1. Cut a strip of felt measuring 1½ inches wide by 16 inches long. **2. To make** the heart, take a piece of wool roving, place it on the foam, and squash it together a little with your fingers. Using the felting needle, poke the wool to make a heart shape. Add little bits of wool as you continue pricking until you get the right shape. **3. Place** the strip of felt on the foam. Center the heart on top and prick through it to fix it to the felt. **4. Take** a thin piece of wool. With the foam underneath, place the wool strip on the felt, to the left of the heart. Use the felting needle to felt the strip of wool and attach it to the felt choker. **5. Glue** the Velcro to each end of the strip of felt to close the choker.

Natural Necklace

YOU WILL NEED:

- a pebble
- a paintbrush
- chocolate-brown acrylic paint
- copper-colored acrylic paint
- a waxed cotton lace or leather cord
- 2 wooden beads

1. Paint the pebble chocolate brown. Leave it to dry. **2. Paint** diagonal copper lines across the pebble. Leave to dry. **3. Double** the cord. Holding the looped end of the cord in place at the top of the pebble, wrap the doubled cord around the pebble and pull the two ends of the cord back through the loop at the top. String a wooden bead over the doubled cord to top of pebble. Make a knot. String the second bead onto the doubled cord and make another knot just above it. **4. Make** a knot to close the necklace to your desired length.

A Button Collar and Bracelet

YOU WILL NEED:

- a tape measure
- grosgrain ribbon (1 inch wide)
- matching cotton thread
- a needle
- small mother-of-pearl buttons
- a metal hook clasp
- heat-seal paper
- cotton ribbon of the same color and width as the grosgrain ribbon
- scissors
- iron

1. Measure the circumference of your neck using the tape measure and add ¾ inch to this length. Sew the mother-of-pearl buttons next to each other onto the grosgrain ribbon, making sure that they are properly aligned. **2. Leave** a margin of ⅓ inch at the beginning and end of the ribbon. When you have covered the entire length of the ribbon, sew each half of the metal hook clasp to each end of the ribbon (⅓ inch from the end). Turn the margins back over the clasp halves and sew them using large stitches. **3. Cut off** a strip of heat-seal paper, as well as a length of matching cotton ribbon, to the same size as the collar. Apply the strip of heat-seal paper to the underside of the collar using an iron on the linen setting (usually the highest temperature setting) but no steam. Remove the protective strip from the heat-seal paper and fix the cotton ribbon to it, still using the iron. The same technique is used to make the bracelet, but it is quicker!

Flower Ring

YOU WILL NEED:

- felt: deep purple and magenta color
- scissors
- fabric glue
- seed beads in shades of red
- red thread
- a needle

1. Trace out the patterns of flowers 1 and 2 on the deep purple felt (*see p. 303*). Cut them out. **2. Trace** out the pattern of flower 2 on the magenta felt. Cut it out. **3. Glue** the three flowers on top of each other in such a way that the petals of one flower sit between those of the flower below. **4. Prepare** a length of thread. Stitch the flowers from below. String five beads onto the thread, pass the thread through the first four of these beads and stitch underneath the flowers. Make a knot. Repeat the operation six times. Make a knot behind the flowers. **5. Cut out** a strip of felt measuring ⅓ inch x 2½ inches. Adjust the size of the felt strip to fit your finger, then glue the two ends together. Sew the flower to the strip of felt.

Beautiful Flower Necklace

YOU WILL NEED:

- thick copper-plated metal wire
- 6 frosted beads (8 mm in diameter)
- 2 black beads (8 mm in diameter)
- 5 amber multifaceted crystal beads (10 mm in diameter)
- a gold-colored crystal pendant (12 mm in diameter)
- 2 black multifaceted beads (8 mm in diameter)
- a large black iridescent oval glass bead
- a gilded metal bead (10 mm in diameter)
- round-nose pliers
- wire cutters
- 40 inches of copper-plated jewelry chain
- 3 copper-plated pierced open-work ring settings (¾ inch in diameter)
- 3 orange flat-bottomed rhinestones (6 mm in diameter)
- gem glue
- a claw setting (8 mm in diameter)
- a rhinestone (8 mm in diameter)
- 40 inches of fancy ribbon (¼ inch)
- 12 inches of plum-colored velvet ribbon (1½ inches wide)
- 12 inches of mustard-colored moiré velvet ribbon (1½ inches wide)
- scissors
- a needle and thread

1. **Thread** each bead onto the metal wire, making a loop at both ends of each bead. **2. Glue** the rhinestones onto the pierced open-work ring settings and leave them to dry. **3. Use** the wire cutters to cut the chain every 2 inches or so in order to add a bead, then close the rings. Spread the various beads out as you assemble the chain. Also add the pierced open-work ring settings. **4. Once** you have completed the assembly, thread the fancy ribbon through the chain every 4 inches. **5. To make** the velvet flower: roughly cut petal shapes (*see p. 304*) from the plum-colored ribbon. Start by cutting out little petals for the heart, followed by the large petals. **6. Begin** by assembling the little petals to form the heart of the flower: stitch them to the ribbon (placing the stitches on the reverse of the ribbon). Continue to add larger and larger petals until you have made a flower about 3 inches wide. **7. Insert** the rhinestone into the setting and close the claws to hold it tight. Now place it in the center of the flower. **8. To make** the leaves: roughly cut the pieces of mustard-colored ribbon (*see p. 304*) and sew them to the underside of the flower. **9. Finish** by fixing the flower to the chain with a few stitches.

Beaded and Buttoned Bracelet

YOU WILL NEED:

- navy-blue cotton fabric
- an embroidery frame
- blue grosgrain ribbon (1 inch wide)
- scissors
- a needle
- matching cotton thread
- seed beads
- 3 blue mother-of-pearl buttons (¾ inch diameter)
- navy-blue cotton ribbon
- a tape measure
- a white mother-of-pearl shoe button

1. Stretch a piece of navy-blue fabric over the embroidery frame. Cut a 7-inch piece from the grosgrain ribbon and baste the edges of the ribbon onto the stretched fabric. **2. Embroider** as many tight lines of beads as required to make a square. Leave an empty space of ¾ of an inch, then embroider another square of beads. **3. Continue** until you have embroidered four squares of beads, then sew the mother-of-pearl buttons into the empty spaces. Remove the stretched fabric from the frame and cut it at just over ½ inch from the edges of the ribbon. **4. Rebaste** the edges of the fabric under the ribbon and cut a 7-inch piece from the navy-blue cotton ribbon. Place this on the back of the grosgrain ribbon and sew them together along the edges using tight little stitches. **5. Turn** back ⅓ inch at each end of the two ribbons. To make the fastening: string seed beads onto a double length of cotton thread. Make a loop at one end and attach the shoe button at the other. **6. Finish** by making a double knot and passing the needle and thread through the thickness of the bracelet. Bring the needle and thread out 1½ inches farther and use the scissors to cut off the excess thread at the level of the fabric.

Personalized Bracelet

YOU WILL NEED:

- a piece of ribbon (grosgrain or velvet, ½ an inch wide)
- a tape measure
- scissors
- matching stranded cotton thread
- 9-hole buttons
- an embroidery needle

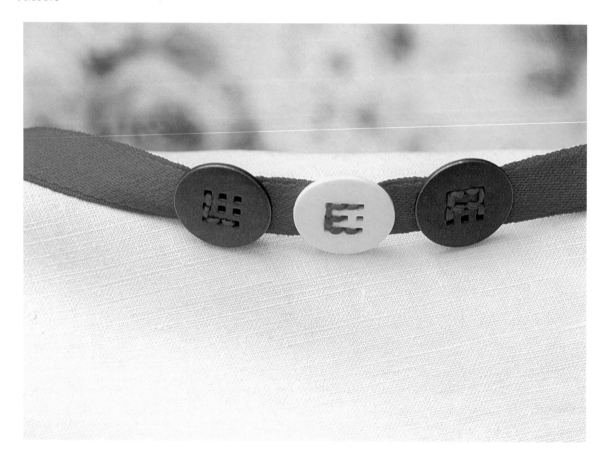

1. Cut a 12-inch length of ribbon. Embroider the buttons with your name, using a back stitch, fixing them to the ribbon as you do so. **2. Start** with the middle letter of the name, making sure that it is placed in the middle of the ribbon. The bracelet simply ties around the wrist.

All Pinned Up

YOU WILL NEED:

- 22 safety pins (¾ inch long)
- black seed beads
- 11 black multifaceted beads (4 mm long)
- flat-nose pliers
- round-nose pliers
- 2 crimp beads
- metallic thread
- 22 black multifaceted beads (5 mm long)
- a jump ring
- a split ring
- a rigid silver-plated neckwire

1. Take 11 safety pins and thread a number of black seed beads onto each of them. Take 10 safety pins and thread three black seed beads, one black multifaceted (4 mm) bead, and two black seed beads. Close the safety pins and use the flat-nose pliers to crimp the heads so that they cannot pop open. **2. Use** the round-nose pliers to unroll the base (opposite the head) of the last safety pin. Thread two crimp beads onto it and push them along until they end up on the part of the pin that has the head on it. Once the beads are on this side, close the base as it was before, crimping it firmly. (Do not crimp the crimp beads at this time.) Thread three black seed beads onto the pin, followed by one black multifaceted (4 mm) bead, and then two black seed beads. Crimp the head as before so that it cannot pop open. **3. Cut** 12 inches of metallic thread. Fold it in half. Thread all of the safety pins onto the doubled thread from the base, starting with the one that has the crimp beads on it. Then alternate one safety pin with only black seed beads on it and one safety pin with a multifaceted bead on it. Pass the surplus metallic thread through the crimp beads on the first safety pin. **4. Take** one of the threads and pass it through the hole in the head of the first safety pin (the one bearing the crimp beads). Thread one multifaceted bead (5 mm) onto the metallic thread, then pass the metallic thread through the head of the second safety pin, thread another multifaceted bead onto it, and continue in this way until the outer circle has been formed. Once you have reached the start again, pass the remaining thread through the crimp beads, then crimp both crimp beads with the pliers. Cut off any excess thread. **5. Thread** the jump ring through the hole in the head of the first safety pin, then attach it to the rigid silver-plated neckwire using the split ring.

Button Wrap Bracelet

YOU WILL NEED:

- cotton cord in a variety of colors
- a tape measure
- scissors
- 40 (approximate) buttons of varying sizes and colors
- large glass beads

1. Cut four lengths of 20 inches and two lengths of 28 inches from the various cords. String the buttons onto them, making a simple knot at the back of each button and placing them 1½ to 2 inches apart. **2. It is** important to place them on the cords in an irregular manner so that they do not cover each other once you have finished the bracelet. String all the large glass beads in one location onto one of the cords in between two buttons. Leave a 4-inch stretch free of buttons at the end of each cord. Link all of the cords together by making a knot 2⅓ inches from the end of the shorter cords and 6⅓ inches from the ends of the longer ones. Tie the cords together in this manner on both ends. **3. Take** the two longest cords at each end and wind one around the ends of the remaining cords (approximately five times) so as to hold them all together. Make a double knot with the other long cord. **4. Tie** the longest two ends in a bow at your desired length. This piece may be worn either as a necklace or a bracelet.

Hoop Necklace

YOU WILL NEED:

- plastic and wooden hoops (use curtain rings, sweater buckles, etc.)
- a mini-drill and drill bits
- a mini-sander
- silver-plated jump rings (7 mm in diameter)
- small pliers

1. Drill a hole through either side of each hoop (slightly off center; see photo). Take care that the off-center axis of the hoops is always on the same side, so that they will hang properly once connected. If any hoop is too thick to hold a ring, use the mini-sander to sand the hoop down a bit. **2. Use** the small pliers to gently open the jump rings and link each hoop to the next one. Mix up the hoops by size, color and shape as you link them together. Variant: link three rectangular hoops together and attach them to a piece of light-brown cord.

Ultra-Chic Ring

YOU WILL NEED:

- thick brass-plated metal wire
- wire cutters
- round-nose pliers
- 45 gilded beads (3 mm in diameter)
- perforated octagonal crystal pendant (12 mm in diameter)
- thin brass-plated metal wire

1. To make the ring itself: use the handle of a tool that has a similar diameter to that of your finger. Roll the thick metal wire around the tool handle in a spiral, making three or four very tight turns. Leave about ⅓ of an inch of wire flat at each end. Cut off the excess with the cutting pliers. **2. Use** the round-nosed pliers to make a small loop at one of the ends. **3. Thread** a sufficient number of gilded beads onto the wire so that it covers this spiral completely, then close the other end with a loop. Make sure that the two end loops line up across the top of the ring. **4. Place** the pendant on top of the ring. Pass the thin metal wire through the holes in the pendant and through the loops on the ends of the ring spirals to fix the pendant to the ring. Cut off any excess wire.

Glass Bead Jewelry

YOU WILL NEED:

To make the ring you will need:

- 2 (8-inch-long) transparent sea-green loopie cords (tubular, hollow plastic lace)
- a glass bead
- scissors
- a ring finding
- glue

To make the bracelet you will need:

- an (8-inch-long) transparent sea-green loopie cord (tubular, hollow plastic lace)
- a glass bead
- scissors
- a clasp

To make the ring: 1. Take the two plastic cords and start a round boondoggle without a starting loop (*see p. 298*); make three stitches. **2. Slip** two cords inside a bead, pull the two others, and continue the braiding. **3. Make** three stitches, tighten well, and cut off the excess. **4. Glue** the bead to the ring finding.

To make the bracelet: 1. String the bead into the middle of an 8-inch plastic cord. **2. Braid** a round four-thread boondoggle (*see p. 297*) on each side of the bead, making three stitches on each. **3. Tighten** the last stitches well and cut off the excess. **4. Knot** the two ends of the bracelet to the two ends of the clasp tightly and cut off the excess.

Ribbon Bracelet

YOU WILL NEED:

- dark pink velvet ribbon (7 inches long and ¼ inch wide)
- brown grosgrain ribbon (7 inches long and 1½ inches wide)
- opaque mauve seed beads
- opaque brown seed beads
- purple stranded embroidery thread (one ply)
- dark pink sewing thread
- brown sewing thread
- Velcro (a self-adhesive piece, about an inch)

1. Place the pink ribbon in the center of the brown ribbon. Attach by sewing a mauve bead and a brown bead together at regular intervals. **2. Create** a bunch of beads in the center by making strings of irregularly mixed mauve and brown beads. Wind the thread around the last bead then pass both needle and thread through all of the beads again. Make a dozen such strings, varying the number of beads each time (between 10 and 15 beads). **3. Make** one star-shaped cross-stitch around each pair of beads and around the bunch of beads (*see p. 296*), using the purple stranded embroidery thread. **4. Overcast** the ends of the ribbon by hand with matching thread. **5. Fix** the two halves of the Velcro piece to the bracelet according to the size of your wrist.

Nefertiti Pendant

YOU WILL NEED:

- thin brass-plated metal wire
- wire cutters
- round-nose pliers
- 75 gilded seed beads
- 9 metal beads (3 mm in diameter)
- 14 metal tube beads
- 3 gilded pierced open-work ring settings (15 mm in diameter)
- 3 rhinestones (3 mm in diameter)
- gem glue
- 5 bronze multifaceted crystal beads (3 mm in diameter)
- 4 gilded jump rings
- tubular metal ribbon

1. **Prepare** five lengths of wire: 2¼ inches; 2 inches; 1½ inches; 1⅓ inches; 1¼ inches. Place them in the order shown in the photo, longest on the bottom, ready to be strung with beads. Make a small loop with the round-nose pliers at one end of the longest wire. 2. **To** make the sides of the triangle, cut two lengths of wire (2⅓ inches long). 3. **Take** short lengths of wire, form a small loop at one end, string a gilded bead onto the wire, then fix the bead in place with a second loop. String each gilded bead and each tube onto individual metal wires in this way. 4. **Glue** the rhinestones onto the pierced open-work ring settings and leave them to dry. 5. **Assembly** of the first metal wire row: in this order string a tube bead bottom loop (so the tube bead is vertical), 4 seed beads, a tube bead bottom loop, 4 seed beads and so on until the end of the row (8 tube beads). Close the end of the bottom wire with a loop. 6. **Assembly** of the second metal wire row: in this order string the other end loop of a tube bead, a seed bead, a metal bead bottom loop, and a seed bead until the end of the row (7 metal beads in all). Finish each end of this wire with a loop. 7. **Assembly** of the third row: in this order string a seed bead, the other end of a metal bead, a seed bead, a tube bead top loop, and a seed bead until the end of the row (6 tube beads in all). Finish each end of this wire with a loop. 8. **Assembly** of the fourth row: in this order string a seed bead, the other end loop of a tube bead, a seed bead, a multifaceted crystal bead bottom loop, and a seed bead until the end of the row (5 multifaceted beads in all). Finish each end of this wire with a loop. 9. **Last** row: string a seed bead and the other end loop of a crystal bead, etc. and close the end of the wire with a loop. 10. **Link** the end of each row to one of the side lengths of metal wire. Add a metal bead on the top of each side, make loops and join these loops with a jump ring. 11. **Use** 3 jump rings to suspend the 3 pierced open-work ring settings from the base of the triangle. 12. **String** the pendant onto the metal ribbon.

Just Splendid

YOU WILL NEED:

- a mini-drill and drill bits
- a red mother-of-pearl button (37 mm in diameter)
- 7 natural mother-of-pearl buttons (22 mm in diameter)
- 6 red mother-of-pearl buttons (22 mm in diameter)
- 2 pink square mother-of-pearl buttons (15 mm on each side)
- 2 pink square mother-of-pearl buttons (10 mm on each side)
- 2 natural mother-of-pearl flower buttons (17 mm in diameter)
- 2 natural mother-of-pearl flower buttons (10 mm in diameter)
- 3 pink mother-of-pearl buttons (15 mm in diameter)
- 2 natural mother-of-pearl buttons (15 mm in diameter)
- silver-plated metal wire
- wire cutters
- 14 silver-plated jump rings (8 mm in diameter)
- round-nose pliers
- 2 pink cotton cords (8½ to 9 inches each)
- 2 small silver-plated crimp beads
- 2 silver-plated cord ends
- flat-nose pliers
- a silver-plated clasp

1. Use the mini-drill to make two holes in the following buttons: the very large red button, the natural mother-of-pearl buttons (22 mm in diameter), and the red mother-of-pearl buttons (22 mm in diameter). Place the holes opposite each other, 2 mm from the edge. **2. Using** the photo above as inspiration, place the remaining various buttons on top of each other and fix them together by passing the silver-plated metal wire through their holes three times. Twist the wire around itself at the back of the buttons and poke the remaining ends through the buttonholes. **3. Using** the round-nose pliers, gently open the jump rings, link all of the button combinations together, closing the jump rings as you go. **4. Take** the pink cords and pass one through each of the rings on the ends of the necklace. Fold each cord in two and slip a small crimp bead onto each one. Place the small crimp bead immediately after the jump ring attached to the top of the last button. Use the flat-nose pliers to crimp the beads. Place a cord end onto the other end of each doubled cord. Attach the cord ends to the ends of the cords using the flat-nose pliers. Attach the cord ends to the clasp.

Avant-garde Pendant

YOU WILL NEED:

- a black plastic salad spoon
- a metal saw
- a small file
- a mini-drill
- 2 large silver jump rings
- round-nose pliers
- a black leather cord
- a clasp

1. Saw off the handle of the plastic salad spoon; make a triangular cut if the object allows it. **2. File** down the plastic edge to make it smooth and soft to the touch. **3. Drill** two holes at the top of the pendant. Open the jump rings using the pliers, pass the rings through the holes in the pendant, and close the jump rings around them. String the leather cord through the rings. Either tie the cord off at your desired length, or, for a shorter length necklace, attach a cord end to each end of the leather cord, crimping each tightly once in place, and attach to the clasp.

Super Rings

YOU WILL NEED:

For the satellite ring you will need:
- nylon thread
- scissors
- a nine-hole button
- seed beads of various sizes
- little crimp beads
- flat-nose pliers
- a fancy button
- an embroidery needle

- a flat ring support
- epoxy glue
- wooden craft stick

For the stack ring you will need:
- fancy buttons of various sizes and colors
- epoxy glue
- a flat ring support

Satellite ring: 1. Cut small lengths of nylon thread and pass the ends of each strand through the holes of the nine-hole button so that the ends are on the topside of the button. String a seed bead sandwiched between 2 crimp beads onto the top end of each of the 18 strands. Crimp the two crimp beads in place with the pliers to hold the decoration at the end of each strand. **2. Center** the fancy button on top of the nine-hole button, fanning the beaded strands around the edge. Attach the fancy button to the nine-hole button by sewing them together with more nylon thread and the embroidery needle. Make a double knot on the top of the fancy button, leaving small lengths of nylon thread coming out of the top. Bead these fancy threads as you did before, with a seed bead sandwiched between 2 crimp beads. **3. Glue** the fancy button onto the nine-hole button with the epoxy glue, spreading the glue in a thin layer with the craft stick. Leave it to dry, then glue the whole piece onto the ring support with the epoxy glue.

Stack ring (not pictured)**: 1. Choose** a range of buttons in contrasted colors and sizes and glue them together from largest to smallest, using the epoxy glue. **2. Glue** the piece onto the ring support using the epoxy glue.

Sun Ring

YOU WILL NEED:

- a round pebble
- acrylic paint: mandarin; orange; pearl orange
- nylon thread
- a perforated ring support
- orange translucent seed beads
- needle
- epoxy glue

1. Paint the pebble in mandarin and leave it to dry. **2. Paint** a pearl orange sun in the middle of the pebble and leave it to dry. (*see p. 304*) **3. Paint** the outside edge of the sun in orange and leave it to dry. **4. Knot** the thread onto an outside hole of the perforated ring support. String 5 beads onto the thread, pass the thread through the first 4 beads again, and knot it onto the ring base. **5. Do** the same for each of the outside holes on the perforated ring support, alternating between 5 and 6 beads per strand of thread. **6. Glue** the painted pebble onto the ring base.

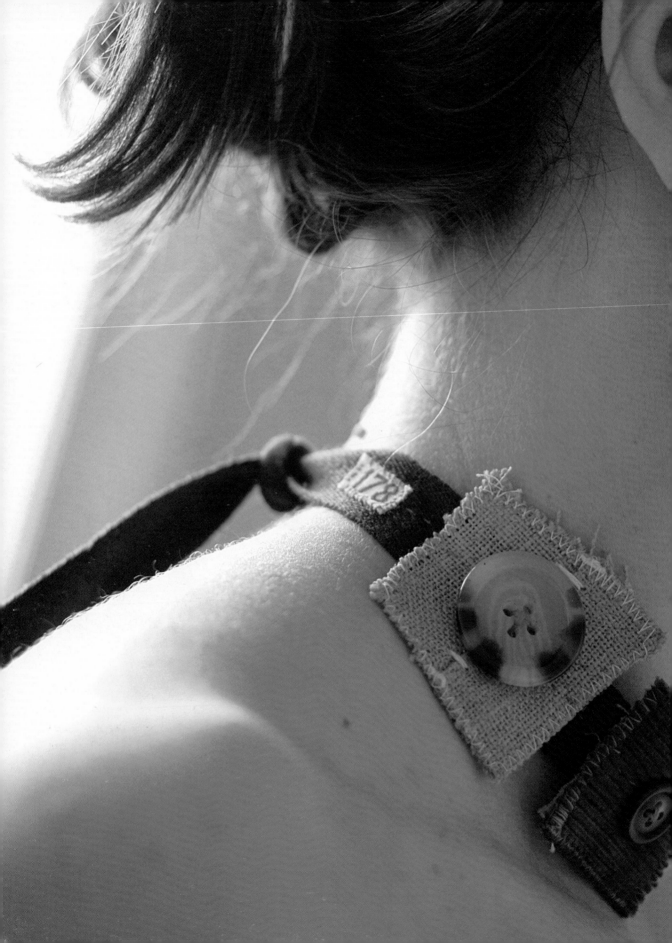

Sampler Necklace

YOU WILL NEED:

- small pieces of linen-twine fabric, boiled wool, and corduroy
- a tape measure
- cotton thread: fuchsia and cream-colored
- a needle
- scissors
- buttons in various sizes made of mother-of-pearl, horn, and light-colored wood
- herringbone ribbon
- a fabric label with embroidered number

1. Cut out 2-inch squares from the various fabrics. Whip stitch the four sides of each square to prevent fraying, using the fuchsia-colored thread for some and the cream-colored thread for others. **2. Sew** a button into the middle of each one using the fuchsia-colored thread. **3. Center** and sew these squares onto the ribbon: pass the thread through the buttons and sew a running stitch along the length of the ribbon. **4. Use** the same thread to sew the number label to the ribbon using gros point stitches. To wear, tie the necklace off at desired length.

Glacier Necklace

YOU WILL NEED:

- 27½ inches of tubular metal ribbon
- 15 light-blue and mauve multifaceted crystal beads (8 mm in diameter)
- 9 transparent drop beads with top wires (4 x 6 mm)
- pliers
- 2 fold-over ends
- spring ring or lobster claw clasp
- jump rings

1. Insert the crystal beads into the tubular ribbon, spacing them out a little. Twist the ribbon between each bead. **2. Using** the pliers, carefully loop each drop bead's top wire around a bit of twisted ribbon between the crystal beads in the center of the necklace (see photo). **3. Finish** by attaching a fold-over end to each end of the ribbon and close with the pliers. Attach end to the clasp, using jump rings.

Fabric Rings

YOU WILL NEED:

For the gray ring you will need:
- a button with rhinestones
- thread
- a piece of pink felt (¾ inch square)
- a piece of gray flannel (3⅛ inches x ¾ inch)
- fabric glue

For the chocolate-brown ring you will need:
- fabric glue
- 4 inches of chocolate-brown satin ribbon (⅓ inch wide)
- a piece of olive-green wool felt (3⅛ inches x ¾ inch)

- a large, flat, brown button
- brown seed beads
- a large round olive-green button

For the pink ring you will need:
- bright-pink felt (3⅛ inches x ¾ inch)
- matching thread
- a large light-green button
- a medium blue button
- a small mauve bead
- 2 small green buttons

Gray ring: 1. Sew the button with rhinestones onto the square of pink felt. **2. Glue** this pink square onto the strip of gray flannel. **3. Close** the ring to fit your finger and use a spot of fabric glue to fasten it.

Chocolate-brown ring: 1. Glue the satin ribbon onto the center of the wool felt. Turn over the excess ribbon at each end and glue it to the underside of the felt. **2. Sew** the large button onto the strip. **3. String** 5 seed beads onto the button, followed by the green bead. Add another 5 seed beads then pass the thread back through the button. **4. Close** the ring to fit your finger and use a spot of fabric glue to fasten it.

Pink ring: 1. Sew the buttons onto the strip of felt. Place the large button onto the middle of the piece, with the medium button on top of it and the small bead on top of that. Place the two small buttons on the sides. **2. Close** the ring to fit your finger and fasten it with a few hand stitches.

Wooden Rings

YOU WILL NEED:

- small twigs of wood (from ⅛ of an inch to 1 inch in diameter)
- a handsaw
- wood glue
- a glue gun and glue sticks
- a ring support (one per ring)
- a small bead

Flower ring: 1. Take a ⅓-inch-thick twig and cut a slice (⅛-inch-thick) from it. Take a ¼-inch-thick twig and cut 5 (⅛-inch-thick) slices from it. **2. Use** the glue gun to fix the 5 little slices onto the ring support, then glue the large slice on top, centering it in the middle of the 5 others.

Sun ring: 1. Take a ⅓-inch-thick twig and cut 8 (⅛-inch-thick) slices from it. **2. Use** the glue gun to fix one of the wood slices to the center of the ring support, then cut the 7 other slices in two. **3. Glue** the 14 half-slices around the central slice.

Straw ring: 1. Take a ⅛-inch-thick twig and cut 5 (1-inch-long) pieces from it. **2. Glue** the 5 pieces together side by side, using a little warm glue. Leave to dry and then glue on top of the ring support.

Bead ring: 1. Take a 1-inch-thick twig and cut a slice (⅛ inch thick) from it. Then take a ⅓-inch-thick twig and cut another ⅛-inch-thick slice. Cut off two sides of the largest wood slice at right angles and attach it to the ring support with the glue gun. **2. Glue** the little slice on top of the large one and glue a little bead on top of that to finish off.

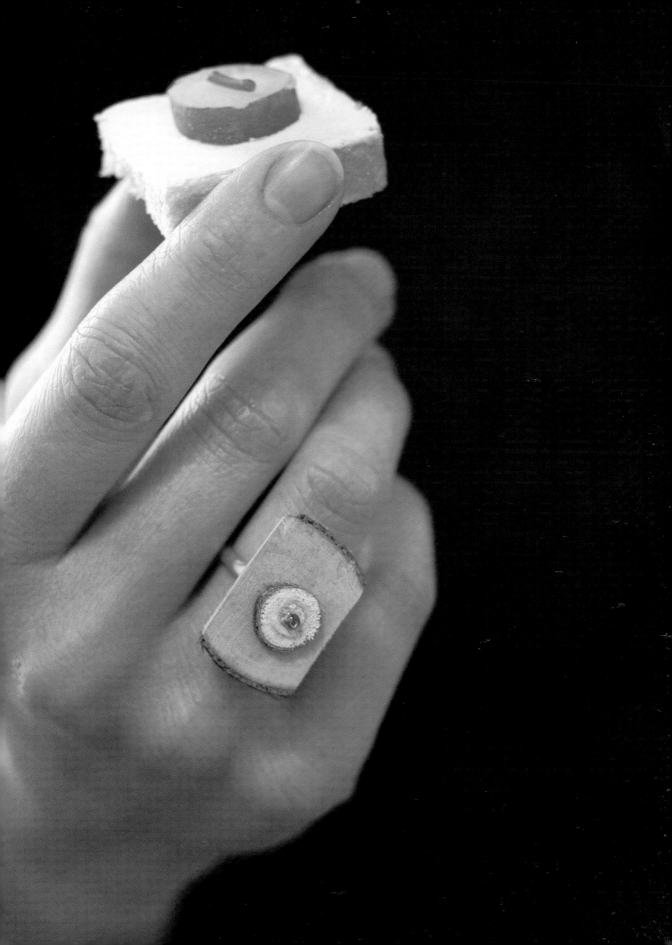

A Matching Set

YOU WILL NEED:

For the necklace you will need:
- 4 loopie cords (tubular, hollow plastic lace): 3 black; 1 gold
- glue
- 3 beads
- glue
- a clasp
- scissors

For the bracelet you will need:
- 4 loopie cords: 2 black; 2 gold

- a bead
- scissors
- a clasp

For the earrings you will need:
- 2 loopie cords: 1 black; 1 gold
- 2 beads
- 2 earring clasps
- scissors
- glue

Necklace: 1. Knot the ends of the four cords together, leaving about 1½ inches free. **2. Braid** a round four-cord boondoggle (*see pp. 297 to 298*). **3. Untie** the knot at the bottom. **4. Braid** the loose ends together, leaving just ¾ of an inch to attach the clasp. **5. Glue** the last stitch. **6. Continue** braiding the other end until you have a length of just over 5 inches. **7. Place** a bead between the four cords and make a stitch to hold it tight. **8. Continue** braiding the boondoggle for another 1¼ inches and add another bead in the same manner. **9. Braid** another 1¼ inches and add the final bead. **10. Continue** braiding for another 5 inches and glue the last stitch. **11. Cut** the ends off two of the cords, knot the other two cords to the clasp, and cut off any surplus. **12. Repeat** for the other side.

Bracelet: 1. Knot the ends of the four cords together. **2. Braid** a round four-lace boondoggle approximately 3¼ inches long. **3. Take** an identical bead to the one you used for the necklace, place it in the center of the bracelet between the four cords and make a stitch to hold it tight. **4. Braid** the boondoggle for another 3¼ inches. **5. Glue** the last stitch. **6. Cut** the ends off two of the cords, knot the other two cords to the clasp, and cut off any surplus. **7. Untie** the first knot and attach the clasp in the same way.

Earrings: 1. Start braiding a round four-cord boondoggle without a starting loop (*see pp. 297 to 298*). **2. Complete** three stitches. **3. Place** a bead between the four cords and make a stitch to hold it tight. **4. Complete** another three stitches. **5. Cut** the ends off two of the cords and knot the other two cords to the earring clasp. **6. Glue**, then cut off any surplus. **7. Repeat** for the other earring.

Metal Web Bracelet

YOU WILL NEED:

- a roll of very fine purple metal wire
- a number 2 crochet hook
- 50 bronze multifaceted beads
  (3 mm in diameter)
- wire cutters
- a double-drilled crystal pendant
  (15 mm in diameter)

1. **Before** you begin the crochet, string the required number of beads onto the wire. You will insert the beads as you progress. **2. Make** a chain of 60 slip stitches (*see p. 296*) or adapt the number of stitches to the size of your wrist. It is best to work with an even number of stitches. **3. Make** the first row without integrating any beads. Make a single crochet on each slip stitch. **4. At** the end of the first row make three slip stitches in order to turn. For the second row make one loop in each crochet. Insert one bead every two loops. **5. The** third row is the same as the second row. **6. The** fourth row is the same as the second row. **7. The** fifth and final row consists of a line of crochets without beads to finish the bracelet. **8. For** the clasp, make an attachment loop, then pass the metal wire through to the middle of the bracelet's width, make a few chain stitches, link to the bracelet with a slip stitch, and then cut the wire. **9. Fix** the crystal pendant to the other end of the bracelet by wrapping metal wire through the side holes on the pendant and the edge of the bracelet.

Squash Queen

YOU WILL NEED:

- small cleaned and dried squash seeds (approximately 30 per ring)
- a mini-drill and drill bits
- acrylic varnish
- a fine paintbrush
- small silver-plated jump rings
- round-nose pliers
- earring hooks
- fine silver-plated chain
- a round perforated silver-plated metal ring support
- very thin nylon thread (¼ mm)
- turquoise-blue acrylic paint
- drop beads

Earrings: 1. Make a hole near the narrow end in each of 6 squash seeds (3 for each earring), using the mini-drill fitted with the narrowest bit. Varnish the seeds, front and back, then leave to dry. **2. Fix** a small jump ring onto each seed, using the pliers, then attach them to three different lengths of chain (from 1¼ to 2 inches). **3. Link** the three chains together with a jump ring and attach the latter to an earring hook.

Natural ring: 1. Make a hole near the narrow end in each squash seed (about 30 seeds total), using the mini-drill fitted with the narrowest bit, centering the hole underneath the point of the seed. **2. Attach** the seeds to the perforated grille of the ring support, starting in the center. Pass the thread through a hole and string one squash seed onto it. Pass the thread back through the same hole to bring it out on the reverse of the grille and then pass it up through the nearest hole. Continue to pass the thread through all of the perforations so as to hide the grille and so that the seeds are packed closely together on the ring support. Pull tightly on the nylon thread as you progress. **3. Knot** the threads underneath and tuck away any excess. **4. Attach** the grille to the ring support by closing the claws, using the flat-nose pliers. **5. Give** the seeds one coat of acrylic varnish to protect them and to deepen their hue.

Blue ring: 1. Proceed as for the natural ring, replacing the acrylic varnish with the turquoise-blue acrylic paint.

Bead ring: 1. Make this ring in the same way as the first two, adding a drop bead between the squash seeds from time to time.

Bracelet or Cuff

YOU WILL NEED:

- green and red flower-print cotton fabric (10½ x 7 inches)
- 10½ inches of red rickrack (⅓ inch wide)
- red thread
- twisted embroidery thread: red, mauve, orange

- heat-seal fabric (10 x 6¼ inches)
- iron
- sewing machine
- 2 matching buttons

1. Mark out a 3¼ inch-wide strip down the central part of the cotton fabric. **2. Sew** the rickrack by hand, ¼ of an inch from the edge of this area, using a discreet tack stitch. Embroider some of the flowers using a straight-stitch on the petals with the red or mauve thread (6 threads) and use French knots for the hearts of the flowers (*see p. 296*) with the orange thread (6 threads). **3. Affix** the piece of heat-bonded fabric to the back of the embroidered area using an old iron. **4. Sew** the two faces of the strip together, ¼ of an inch from the edge, along the two longer sides but only along one of the shorter sides. Turn the piece over and iron it, centering the seam as you do so. **5. Use** a sewing machine to make the buttonhole, placing it about 1½ inches from one of the shorter edges, according to the size of your wrist. **6. Sew** one button onto the other side of the bracelet, at the same distance from the shorter edge as the buttonhole. Sew the other button onto the rear, in exactly the same place. **7. Use** a discreet tack stitch to close off the last shorter edge by hand.

Romantic Ring

YOU WILL NEED:

- 4 (36-inch) transparent pink loopie cords (tubular, hollow plastic lace)
- scissors
- glue
- a silver-plated metal open-work plate
- a silver-plated metal ring support

1. Cut the 4 cords in the middle and braid a square eight-cord boondoggle without a loop (*see pp. 297 to 300*). **2. Braid** 9 stitches, or as many stitches as required for the boondoggle to be well visible once the plate has been placed on top of it. **3. Cut** off the excess cord and glue the plate squarely in the center. **4. Glue** the ring support to the boondoggle and hold it firmly in place while it dries.

Charming Button Bracelet

YOU WILL NEED:

(Not all of these items are required for one bracelet. These materials are for different methods of making this charm bracelet. Read the complete directions to determine exactly which materials you will require.)

- silver-plated metal chain with large links
- fancy buttons (various shapes, colors, sizes)
- silver-plated metal jump rings (¼ inch in diameter)
- silver-plated metal hooks
- round-nose pliers
- fancy charms and sequins
- beading wire
- wire cutters
- small crimp beads
- flat-nose pliers
- silver-colored seed beads
- nylon thread
- a clasp
- a tape measure

1. Hang the fancy buttons onto your chain using the silver-plated metal jump rings or hooks. Use the round-nose pliers to open a jump ring slightly, slip the ring through the button hole, slip the ring through a link in the chain, then close the ring to secure all. If the button is too thick to hold both the button and the link to the chain, add a second jump ring to allow some dangle. Use the same technique to hang the charms and sequins between them. You may also replace each jump ring or hook with a small length of beading wire held in place with a crimp bead. For this method, insert a small crimp bead onto each wire, string the button or charm onto the wire, loop the wire back through the chain then back on itself, pulling it through the crimp bead every time it passes it. Use the flat-nose pliers to crimp the bead closed and use the wire cutters to trim any excess wire. **2. If you** do not have a chain then make one using the seed beads: take one long piece of nylon thread and fold it in half. String 10 seed beads onto the folded nylon threads, then pass the two excess threads through the hole of the last bead, crossing them as you do so. **3. String** four beads onto one of the nylon threads and six beads onto the other one. Pass the thread bearing the smaller number of beads through the hole of the sixth bead on the other thread, crossing them again. Continue in this way until you have created a chain that is about 7 inches long. **4. Use** a single small crimp bead to close the chain. Use the silver-plated jump rings to attach the clasp onto the bracelet, then hang as many buttons and charms on it as you wish, using the technique described previously.

Button Bracelet

YOU WILL NEED:

- hemp string
- a tape measure
- scissors
- a medium to large button

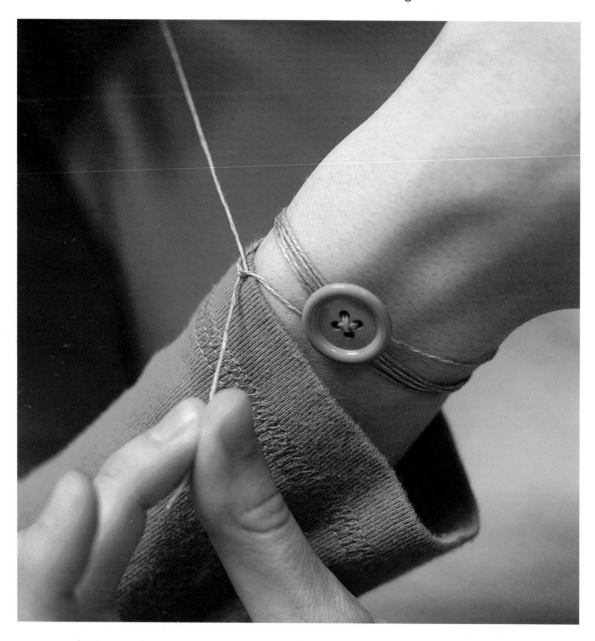

1. Cut a 20-inch length of hemp string. Thread the string through the buttonholes several times so that it is pulled tightly into place. **2. Wind** the string around your wrist several times and knot it, centering the button above the middle of your hand.

Beads and a Button

YOU WILL NEED:

- 8 (12-inch) lengths of beading wire
- a 2-hole mother-of-pearl button (35 mm or 1¼ inches in diameter)
- thin transparent tape
- seed beads
- 2 jump rings
- a split ring
- a clasp
- 14 crimp beads
- flat-nose pliers
- wire cutters

1. Pass all seven lengths of beading wire up through one of the button holes and back down through the other. Center the button in the middle of the wires and put a piece of tape to one side to prevent the button from moving along the wires. **2. Beginning** on the side of the button without the tape, fill the seven lengths of wire with seed beads until you have covered enough to wrap halfway around your wrist with the button centered in the top. (Note that the clasp and rings will add approximately ¾ of an inch to the final length of the bracelet.) There should be excess wire after the final bead. Place a piece of scotch tape at the end of each beaded strand to hold it until you are ready to crimp. **3. Remove** the tape from the side of the centered button and fill those seven lengths of wire with seed beads until it matches the opposite side. Tape each strand as you complete it to make sure the beads do not slide off. To make sure the beaded wires (on both sides) are equal in length, you can either count the number of beads (use approximately 50 per strand per side if using 8/0 seed beads) or measure the beaded strand (between 3 and 4 inches, depending on your wrist circumference if using smaller or mixed-size seed beads). **4. Attach** a jump ring to the clasp. On one side of the bracelet, remove the tape from one of the strands and pass the end of the beaded wire strand through a crimp bead, then through the jump ring attached to the clasp, then back through the crimp bead to form a small loop. Make sure to push all the beads tightly toward the center of the bracelet, then use the flat-nose pliers to tighten the crimp bead at the top of the beads leaving a small loop between the crimp bead and the jump ring so that the strands of beads can move slightly. Repeat this process until all seven beaded strands are attached to the jump ring and are crimped in place on this side of the bracelet. Attach the split ring to the second jump ring. Repeat the same crimping process on the other side of the bracelet, but pull each strand through a crimp bead, through a split ring, and back through the crimp bead before closing in the same manner. **5. To finish** the bracelet, thread about an inch of excess wire from each strand back through the beads, then use the wire cutters to clip off any remaining wire.

Hedgehog Bracelet

YOU WILL NEED:

- stretch nylon thread (16-20 inches)
- thin silk thread
- a small needle

- a large mix of beads (maximum diameter 14 mm)
- scissors
- a candle

1. Double the stretch nylon thread and size it to fit your wrist snugly. Secure the threads with a series of firmly tied knots. **2. The principle** for stringing the beads is always the same: take the silk thread and string one small bead onto it, followed by one medium bead and one larger bead. Pass this thread under the doubled nylon thread and then back through the three beads. Make a very secure double or triple knot on top of the small bead, ensuring that the beads are pulled tight against each other to make the whole piece rigid, then cut the thread. **3. Attach** another string of three beads in the same way ¼ of an inch farther along on the nylon thread, then continue attaching more sets of three beads, always ensuring that the beads are pulled tight, until you have filled the whole bracelet. **4. Once** you have finished the bracelet, cut off the remaining ends of thread at ⅛ of an inch, then melt the ends with a candle to prevent the knots from coming undone. The bracelet should carefully stretch over your hand and onto your wrist.

Wire Loops and Coral

YOU WILL NEED:

- thick brass-plated metal wire
- a pencil
- wire cutters
- 8 brass-plated jump rings of ¼-inch diameter (or make them using the thick brass-plated wire)
- round-nose pliers
- 2 blue drop beads
- 4 round pieces of coral
- 2 large jump rings
- a pair of gilded earring clasps

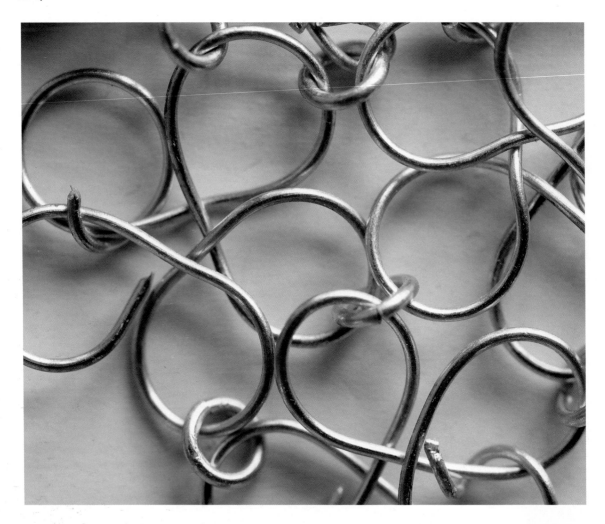

1. Make three spirals by winding the metal wire around a pencil tightly five times for each spiral. Cut the wire leaving a little excess at the end of each spiral. **2. Delicately** flatten the spirals so that they form flower shapes (see close-up photo). **3. Place** the flowers next to each other so that they form a triangle and link them together with the jump rings (use 4 jump rings per earring). **4. Hang** each bead and each piece of coral on a short loop of metal wire and suspend them from the bottom loop-work. Make sure to tighten each loop at the top so the beads do not drop off. **5. Use** the two large jump rings to attach each earring to a clasp.

For My Little Treasure

YOU WILL NEED:

- a length of ribbon embroidered with the child's name
- a tape measure
- scissors
- round-nose pliers
- a large silver-plated metal ring
- a purple mother-of-pearl heart-shaped sequin
- a little plain mother-of-pearl star-shaped button

1. Cut a 10-inch-long piece of embroidered ribbon. **2. Use** the pliers to open the ring, string the heart-shaped sequin and the star-shaped button onto the ring, and close the ring securely again. **3. Pull** the length of ribbon half way through the ring to finish. Tie the small bracelet around the child's wrist.

Felt Flowers

YOU WILL NEED:

- thick dark pink felt
- a pencil
- scissors
- a needle
- dark pink and purple thread
- flat pink sequins
- red seed beads
- fabric glue
- a beautiful wide ribbon

1. Enlarge the flower design (*see p. 301*) by photocopying it and trace its shape twice onto the felt with the pencil. Cut out the flowers. **2. Start** by sewing the two cut flowers together, one centered on top of the other with the petals staggered. Then in the center of the top flower, sew on the sequins with a little seed bead placed in the center of each one. Sew a few more beads around the sequins. **3. Now** make a few long decorative stitches on the felt petals. Sew or glue the flower onto the ribbon.

Variant: Felt flowers with beads for espadrilles.

Checkered Headband

YOU WILL NEED:

- pink-and-white checked cotton
- scissors
- a tape measure
- pins
- iron
- matching cotton thread
- sewing machine
- gathering thread

1. Cut a rectangle measuring 10 x 20 inches from the fabric. Adjust this to fit your head and to the desired width. **2. Pin,** then with an iron press a narrow hem along each side, then stitch. **3. Overcast** the two widths using a sewing machine to prevent fraying. **4. Sew** a gathering stitch across the two ends of the headband and gather to reduce the width to 2 inches. Flatten the ends and press the pleats with a hot iron. **5. Photocopy** the pattern at 100% (*see p. 301*). Cut out and pin the paper to the fabric. Add an extra ⅓ inch around the edge for the hems and cut out the shape. Repeat in order to make the two ties. **6. Pin,** then with an iron press a narrow hem on each of the four sides of the ties. **7. Pin** back the hems on the two long sides of the headband and on the small width on each of the ties. **8. Pin** down the edges without hems on the widths (gathered) of the rectangle. Machine stitch.

Marine Key Ring

YOU WILL NEED:

- 3 pebbles (approximately 1½ to 2½ inches long)
- acrylic paint: navy-blue, sky-blue, turquoise, white, yellow, brown, red, black
- a small plastic wiggly eye
- 3 slightly stiff cords: 1 navy-blue; 1 sky-blue; 1 turquoise (approximately 24 inches in length)
- scissors
- glue
- a metal key ring

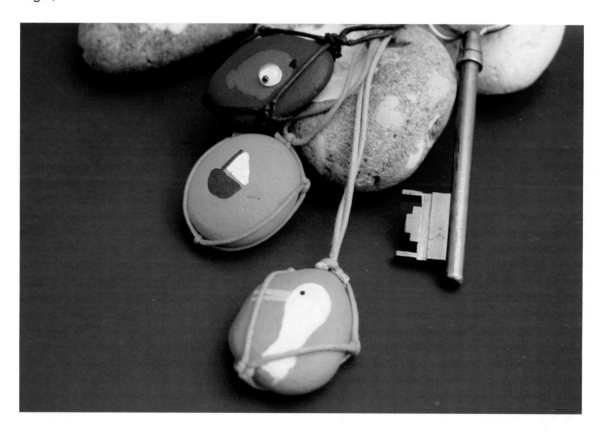

1. Paint the pebbles: one in navy-blue, one in sky-blue, and one in turquoise. Leave them to dry. **2. Using** the patterns on page 301, paint the designs onto the pebbles: Take the navy-blue pebble and paint the goldfish; leave it to dry. Paint in the black mouth; leave it to dry. Glue on the eye. Take the sky-blue pebble: paint the seagull's head; leave it to dry. Paint in the yellow beak and the black eye; leave it to dry. Take the turquoise pebble: paint the brown boat; leave it to dry. Paint in the white sail; leave it to dry. **3. Tie** each lace around the corresponding colored pebble: Cut each lace in two. Cross the two laces and make a knot at the base of the pebble. Take two laces up each side of the pebble, cross them again and knot them. Continue to the top of the pebble, cross them again and knot them. Now knot the four laces together. Put a spot of glue on this last knot to strengthen it. Leave it to dry. **4. On each** pebble, cut two of the laces down to the knot, leaving only two free. **5. Knot** the six laces from the three pebbles together at different heights. Attach the key ring, then your keys.

Flat Elastic Headband

YOU WILL NEED:

- flower-print cotton fabric (20 x 7 inches plus 2 x 4 inches)
- sewing machine
- pins
- iron
- 3¼ inches of elastic (⅓ inch in diameter)
- scissors
- matching cotton thread
- a needle

1. Overcast the pieces of fabric to prevent fraying, using the sewing machine. Pin the lengths of each rectangle right sides together. Front-stitch a seam ⅓ of an inch from the cut edge with the sewing machine. **2. Turn** over the resulting tubes and press them, using a hot iron, and centering the seam. Turn in the edges of the widths on the widest tube. Press the pleats with a hot iron. **3. Slip** the elastic into the small tube and attach the ends with pins, folding over the fabric. **4. Pin** the elastic and its envelope in the center of the openings in the headband. Machine stitch it. Make several overlaid stitches to properly attach and strengthen the ensemble. **5. Fold** the corners of the headband onto the reverse and attach them using small hand stitches.

Nature Rayogram

YOU WILL NEED:

- white or yellow poplin fabric
- a tape measure
- scissors
- cardboard
- UV–sensitive paint (e.g. Setacolor)

- a flat paintbrush
- dried leaves or flower petals
- a sheet of glass (optional)
- corded cotton thread
- an embroidery needle

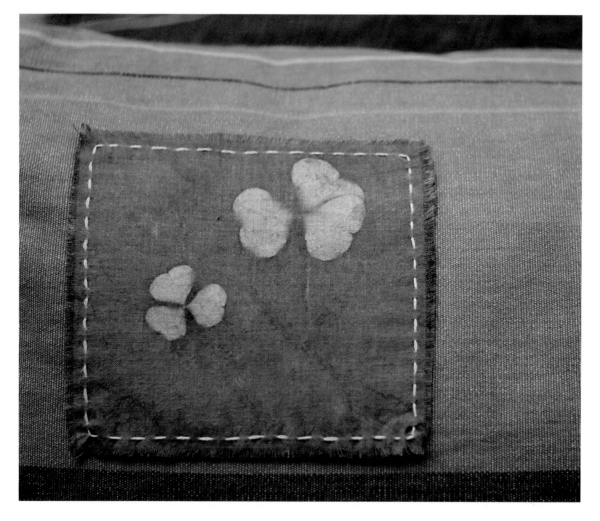

1. Cut three 4-inch squares from the poplin and fray their edges to a thickness of ¼ of an inch. Dampen the squares of fabric with water and place them down flat on a piece of cardboard. Apply a coat of the UV-sensitive paint to each square using a flat paintbrush. Arrange a dried leaf (fern, clover, geranium, etc.) on each piece of fabric. **2. Dry** the pieces of fabric in a well-lit and dust-free place. If you do this outside, make sure that you lay a sheet of glass on top to keep the dried leaves in place. **3. After** the fabric has dried completely, remove the leaves and sew a border along the edges of the squares using a long stitch. Use as a decorative accent on clothing, bags, pillows, etc.

A Touch of Lace

YOU WILL NEED:

- a khaki jacket
- cloth tape measure
- black lace
- scissors
- iron
- pins
- black and khaki-colored thread
- sewing machine

1. Use the cloth tape measure to measure the circumference of the jacket's sleeves, waist, and collar. Cut pieces of lace to fit these areas, adding an extra inch all around. **2. With** the iron, turn up 1/3 of an inch on the lace and press the pleat. Pin the pieces of lace onto the jacket. Straight-stitch the pieces of lace onto the jacket, following the scalloped edges. **3. Take** particular care to place the pieces of lace on the sleeves in a symmetrical manner.

Flower Belt

YOU WILL NEED:

- a cloth belt
- presewn embroidered canvas
- scissors
- pins
- matching thread
- sewing machine

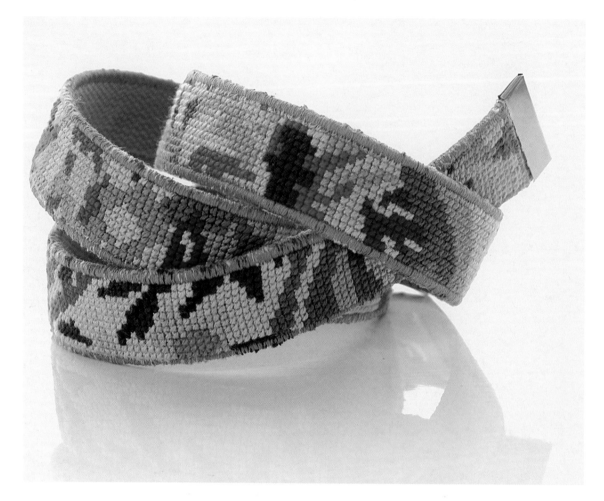

1. Remove the buckle by lifting up the metal clip. **2. Cut** one or several strips from the embroidered canvas the same width as the belt. Place them all along the belt, one after another. **3. Sew** the canvas onto the belt using tight zigzag stitching. Cut off any excess thread. Stitch the edge a second time if necessary.

Little Flower

YOU WILL NEED:

- a pink mother-of-pearl button (1 inch wide)
- an embroidered flower on thick canvas
- 5 heart-shaped natural mother-of-pearl buttons
- pink cotton thread
- a needle
- nylon thread
- little crimp beads
- 2 pebble beads
- mauve metallic tube beads
- mauve and pink seed beads
- flat-nose pliers
- a brooch pin (1 inch wide)
- scissors

1. Sew the pink button onto the center of the flower and the heart-shaped buttons onto the petals, using the pink cotton thread. String one crimp bead, one pebble bead, and about seven tube beads onto the nylon thread. **2. Pass** the nylon thread through the eye of the needle and sew through the central button. Bring the nylon thread out of the front of the flower through the other buttonhole and string about 7 tube beads, 1 pebble bead, and 1 crimp bead onto it. Crimp the crimp beads closed with the flat-nose pliers. **3. Take** another length of nylon thread and repeat the operation, this time replacing the tube beads and pebble beads with the mauve and pink seed beads. Sew the brooch pin onto the back of the flower, using the pink cotton thread.

Black and White

YOU WILL NEED:

- a felted wool beret
- a pencil
- a foam cushion (a piece of dense foam rubber, 1½–2 inches thick)
- black carded wool roving and/or top
- a felting needle

1. **Draw** the swirls (*see p. 302*) on the beret in pencil. 2. **Place** the beret over the foam. Prepare a thin piece of wool roving by shaping it with your fingers. Place it over one of the swirls and poke it into place and shape with the needle, taking care to follow the shape you have drawn. Be sure to insert and remove the needle at the same angle and never twist the needle. Poke the swirls enough to make sure they are firmly attached to the beret. 3. **Repeat** the felting process for the other swirls.

Jeweled Hairstick

YOU WILL NEED:

- a plain, wooden hairstick with four flat sides
- contact glue
- 25 rhinestones (6 mm in diameter) in orange, fuchsia, and red
- red and blue tube beads

1. Place little drops of glue along the part of the hairstick that you wish to decorate and place six flat-back crystals one by one (from the lightest in color to the darkest) with three tube beads between each one. **2. Repeat** for each side of the hairstick, keeping the same order of colors as you work your way around. **3. Finish** by gluing the last crystal onto the end of the hairstick. Make sure that the glue dries properly.

ONLY IN A*
Jeep.

Buttoned

YOU WILL NEED:

- a button-making machine
- a pencil
- scissors
- paper with printed patterns (wrapping paper or crafting paper)
- dried flowers
- dried leaves

1. Cut out disks or rectangles, using the plastic stencils supplied with the button-making machine. **2. Draw** shapes on the paper with a pencil and cut them out. **3. Take** a shape, place it in the machine, put a dried flower or a leaf on top of it in the desired position, then place a sheet of the protective plastic film (supplied with the machine) on top. **4. Press** with the machine to seal. Repeat process for more buttons.

Sequined Brooch

YOU WILL NEED:

- bright pink sequins
- turquoise sequins
- green and bright-pink seed beads
- turquoise thread
- a needle

- plain turquoise cotton fabric (4 x 40 inches)
- striped turquoise cotton fabric (6⅓ x 10 inches)
- a brooch pin (or a safety pin)

1. Set aside 5 pink sequins, 11 turquoise sequins, 5 green beads, and 11 pink beads. **2. Attach**, with a needle and thread, several sequins to one half of the piece of plain turquoise cotton fabric, with the green beads holding the pink sequins in place and the pink beads holding the turquoise sequins in place. **3. Fold** the two pieces of fabric in half lengthways. Pass a gathering thread along the three cut sides of each of the two pieces, pulling the ends together. **4. Close** off the resulting flower by sewing the ends of the fabric together with a few hand stitches. Place the plain turquoise flower inside the striped flower. **5. Make** the heart of the flower: Use the green beads to attach the pink sequins in the center, then use pink beads to attach the turquoise sequins around them, making sure that you run the stitches through the two fabrics. **6. Sew** the brooch/safety pin to the back of this flower.

Flower Barrette

YOU WILL NEED:

- felt: bright green, bright pink
- scissors
- a needle
- green cotton embroidery floss
- pink thread
- craft glue
- a barrette

1. **Draw** three leaf patterns (*see p. 301*) on the green felt, then cut them out. Embroider the central vein with the green floss, using a front stitch. 2. **Draw** the flower pattern (*see p. 301*) on the pink felt, then cut it out. Roll the strip, making a pointed pistil with a ruff around it. Use one or two stitches of the pink thread to hold the shape in place. 3. **Sew** or glue the three leaves onto the end of the ruff in staggered rows. 4. **Glue** the flower onto the barrette.

Cozy Wrap

YOU WILL NEED:

- flower-print cotton fabric (60 x 20 inches)
- brown fake fur or fleece (60 x 20 inches)
- pins
- sewing machine
- matching thread
- scissors
- iron
- a needle

1. Pin the pieces of cotton fabric and fake fur right sides together. Stitch them together ⅓ of an inch from the edge, leaving a stretch of 12 inches unstitched in the center of one of the edges. **2. Turn** inside out through the opening. Press the flower-print side with an iron, making the corners as flat as possible. **3. Hand stitch** the opening closed.

Button Brooches

YOU WILL NEED:

- several sizes of mother-of-pearl buttons
- brooch pins of the same widths as the buttons
- matching cotton embroidery floss
- an embroidery needle
- scissors

1. Use the embroidery floss and an embroidery needle to sew the buttons to the brooch pins. Pass the floss through the buttonholes several times and tighten well. Finish by making a double knot on the back of each pin.

Floral Gloves

YOU WILL NEED:

- raspberry-colored carded wool roving and/or top
- a foam cushion (a piece of dense foam rubber, 1½ to 2 inches thick)
- a felting needle
- pink carded wool roving and/or top
- a pair of yellow wool gloves

1. Take a little of the raspberry wool. Shape it with your fingers, place it on the foam, and poke it with the needle into the shape of one petal. **2. Take** another little piece of wool, shape another petal, and poke it into the base of the first petal. Repeat the operation until you have made a flower with five petals. **3. Take** a little of the pink wool, shape it with your fingers, place it in the center of the flower, and poke it in place. **4. Make** a second flower following the same needle felting process. **5. To attach** the flowers to the gloves insert the foam into the first glove so that it is positioned underneath the flower placement. Needle felt the flower into place. Repeat with the second glove and flower. You may have to sew the felted flowers to the gloves, depending on the mesh of the gloves.

Tortoise Brooch

YOU WILL NEED:

- light-green carded wool roving and/or top
- a foam cushion (a piece of foam rubber, 1½ to 2 inches thick)
- a felting needle
- green carded wool roving and/or top
- a sewing needle
- light-green thread
- two metalized black beads
- light-green tube beads
- glue
- a brooch pin

1. To make the body: take the light-green wool and shape it with your fingers. Place it on the foam and poke it into the shape of a large oval ball using the felting needle. (The longer you poke the wool, the firmer your finished piece will be.) Take the darker green wool, place it on the foam and poke it into a somewhat flat oval (to mimic the tortoise shell). Place it on the felted light-green ball and poke it into place. Take a tiny bit of light-green wool and form really small balls between your fingers. Place each shaped ball on the green wool, and with the foam cushion underneath, poke to felt them. Finally poke them into place to attach to the shell. **2. Head and feet:** take a really small amount of light-green wool, shape four small tortoise foot shapes and one slightly larger head shape with your fingers. Using the foam underneath, poke the pieces with the felting needle to felt them. Attach them in their appropriate spots on the tortoise body by poking them into place. **3. Using** the sewing needle and light-green thread, sew the two black metalized beads in place for the eyes. Sew the tube beads into place as decoration for the tortoise's spots. **4. Glue** the brooch pin onto the belly of the tortoise.

Button Brooch with Ribbons

YOU WILL NEED:

- 8 inches each of 6 kinds of ribbon of different widths, colors, and materials
- a needle and thread
- matte finish olive-green mother-of-pearl 4-hole button (1½ inches in diameter)
- thin nylon thread
- 6 amethyst-colored spinning-top crystal beads
- scissors
- a brooch pin
- glue (optional)

1. Fold one ribbon back on itself to form a kind of loop in the center of which the button will sit. Attach the ribbon to the button with a few stitches. Attach the second ribbon diagonally in the same way. Place each of the remaining ribbons in the same way, with equal spacing between each one, so that their colors and positions are balanced. **2. Bring** a piece of nylon thread up through one buttonhole and string two beads onto it, then pull the thread through the opposite buttonhole to attach them to the center of the button. **3. Pull** the same nylon thread up through a different buttonhole and string 4 beads onto it. Then bring the thread through the final hole and tighten it to secure all beads to the top center of the button. **4. Finish** by sewing or gluing the brooch pin to the back of the brooch.

Fall Scarf

YOU WILL NEED:

- orange carded wool roving and/or top
- a foam cushion (a piece of dense foam rubber, 1½ to 2 inches thick)
- a felting needle
- red carded wool roving and/or top
- natural-colored carded wool roving and/or top
- a brown knitted wool scarf

1. **Take** a piece of orange wool roving. Shape it roughly into a small thumbprint shape with your fingers. Place it on the cushion and poke it with the felting needle to give enough volume so that it becomes almost rounded. 2. **Take** another piece of the same colored wool, shape it with your fingers as before, place it next to the previous piece so that it overlaps, and poke it into shape and attach to the first. 3. **Do** this five times in all to form the wings of the orange leaf (see photos). Prick the last piece into the shape of a stalk. 4. **Do** the same to make the other two leaves, repeating steps one to three. 5. **Place** the needle-felted leaves on one end of the scarf, approximately 6 inches from the edge. Place the foam directly underneath where you plan to needle felt the leaves in place. Again using the felting needle, poke the leaves to the scarf to attach. You may have to sew the leaves in place, depending on the mesh of the scarf.

Ribbon Belt

YOU WILL NEED:

- cotton fabric (30 x 9 inches)
- sewing machine
- pins
- matching cotton thread
- iron
- plain ribbon (½ inch wide and 2 yards and 6 inches long)
- a needle

1. Overcast the piece of fabric on a sewing machine to prevent fraying. **2. Pin** the two long sides with right sides together. **3. Sew** them ⅓ inch from the side, using a front stitch. **4. Turn** the resulting tube inside out and press it with a hot iron, centering the seam. **5. Turn** in the edges of the ends and press the pleats with a hot iron. **6. Cut** the ribbon into equal halves and pin one of them in the center of each short side, leaving an excess of ½ inch inside. Machine stitch. **7. Sew** a little hem by hand at the ends of the ribbons.

Rosette Brooch

YOU WILL NEED:

- lime-green grosgrain ribbon (1½ inches wide x 15 inches long)
- gathering thread
- orange embroidery thread
- turquoise-colored embroidery thread
- a large orange button
- lime-green embroidery thread
- a brooch pin (or a safety pin)

1. Hold the two ends of the ribbon together to create a rosette shape. Stitch a gathering thread along one of the edges and pull the rosette tight. Make a knot. **2. Make** French knots (*see p. 296*) with the orange and turquoise embroidery threads (six threads). **3. Sew** the button into the center of the rosette, using the green thread. **4. Fix** the brooch pin to the back of the rosette with a few stitches.

Feather Brooch

YOU WILL NEED:

- 4 loopie cords (tubular, hollow plastic lace): 3 red, 1 yellow
- a gilded stickpin
- a large yellow bead
- 2 red feathers
- scissors

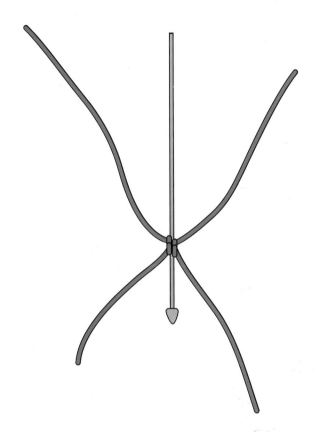

1. Start to braid a four-cord round boondoggle (*see pp. 297 to 300*), using two red cords, placing the stickpin at the center. You should begin the boondoggle at the center of the stickpin. **2. Make** five stitches, add the third red cord to the middle, and increase from four to six cords. Continue to braid around until the spiral has completed one turn. **3. Add** the yellow cord to the center and increase from six to eight cords; make a stitch. **4. Slip** the bead onto the stickpin and the feathers into the bead. **5. Pull** the eight cords above the bead and continue the round boondoggle, making sure that the bead and the feathers remain properly in the center. **6. Stop** braiding when the top of the stickpin has disappeared completely underneath the boondoggle and only the feathers are still visible. **7. Tighten** well and cut off any excess cord.

Pom-pom Keychain

YOU WILL NEED:

- light cardboard
- a pencil
- scissors
- chocolate-colored cotton fabric (23½ x 8 inches)
- olive-green linen fabric (23½ x 8 inches)
- blue-gray satin fabric (23½ x 8 inches)
- 8 inches of light-pink satin ribbon (¼ inch wide)
- an orange leather lace (1 yard long)
- glass beads: brown, olive-green, white
- 4 inches of blue-gray velvet ribbon (½ inch wide)
- a pin
- a tapestry needle
- a little spherical bell
- a keychain carabiner

1. Photocopy the pom-pom shape at 100% (*see p. 305*). Trace the shape out twice on a piece of cardboard (a shoebox, for example) and cut them out. **2. Cut** out a dozen long strips (less than ⅓ inch wide) from the various pieces of fabric. **3. Start** the pom-pom with these strips. Put the two donut-shaped cardboard circles together and begin to wind the fabric strips around, from the outside and up through the inside holes and back around. Cut out more strips of material as you progress with the work. **4. When** the center hole is full, cut the fabric around the rings by gently slipping the point of the scissors again between the two cardboard disks. You may not be able to cut all at once, so just do it a few times. This will create the rough-edged pom-pom shape. Use the point of the scissors to push the leather lace between the two pieces of cardboard, wrap it all the way around, pull it tight, and knot it. Cut each cardboard disk from outer edge to the center hole and remove it from the pom-pom. **5. String** two beads onto the lace. Make a hole in each end of the velvet ribbon with a pin, then widen a little with the tapestry needle. Pass the leather lace through the two holes so as to form a loop of ribbon. **6. String** other beads onto the lace and finish with the little spherical bell. Make several knots to keep the beads and bell in place. **7. Knot** the lace to the carabiner.

Dragonfly Wrap

YOU WILL NEED:

- light-green felt
- scissors
- purple wool felt (1⅓ yards x 1½ yards)
- pins
- sewing machine
- light-green thread
- 20 pink multifaceted beads
- a needle

1. Trace the dragonfly pattern (*see p. 307*) on the light-green felt ten times, then cut out the felt shapes. **2. Place** the dragonflies on the purple felt, spaced out at regular intervals. Use pins to keep them in place. **3. Use** the sewing machine to make three lines of stitches on each dragonfly: two down the center of each pair of wings and the third running from the top of the head to the tip of the tail. **4. Sew** on two beads for the eyes. Repeat for each of the dragonflies on the wrap.

The Key to Happiness

YOU WILL NEED:

- large dry white beans
- a mini-drill and drill bits
- hemp string
- scissors
- a pointed wool needle
- little spherical bells
- beads
- small felted wool balls
- large shaped sequins
- ribbons
- little silver-plated jump rings
- round-nose pliers
- a heart-shaped mother-of-pearl sequin

1. Use the mini-drill to make holes in the center of the large beans. Thread a good length of hemp string onto the wool needle (about 24 inches) and attach a little spherical bell about 2 inches from the end of the string with a double knot. Keep the end of the string free underneath the knot and string the beads, the felted wool balls, the large sequins, and the beans onto the hemp. **2. Finish** with a felted wool ball and make a knot at the top of the ball to keep everything in place. Leave 5 inches of string free, then make another knot on the ball (this will leave a 2½-inch-long loop on top of the ball). Run the string through the ball again and take it out underneath the ball. **3. String** more beans and beads onto the hemp and finish with a little spherical bell. Make a double knot on the bell's ring and pass the hemp once more through the beans or felt balls just above the bell to secure the end. Trim off any excess string. Take the 2 inches of free string that you left underneath the first knot and thread it onto the needle, then pass it through the beads and balls just above it. Cut off any excess thread that sticks out from a bead or ball. **4. Use** the jump rings and round-nose pliers to attach large sequins and the heart-shaped mother-of-pearl sequin onto the little spherical bells.

Little Bead Man

YOU WILL NEED:

- thick silver-plated metal wire (approximately 20 inches total)
- wire cutters
- a selection of fancy glass beads of various sizes and shapes
- round-nose pliers
- a key ring

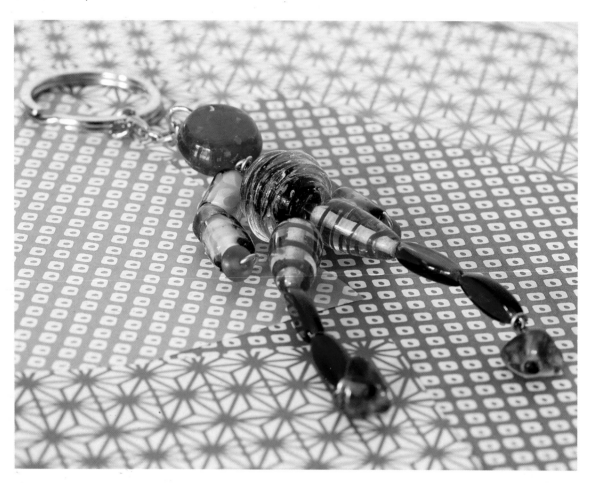

1. Cut approximately 10 inches of metal wire and bend it in half. (The bent wire will serve as a loop at the top of the bead that will be the head and split to form two legs at the bottom). **2. Holding** these two wires together, string one round bead for the head, followed by one large bead for the body. Then string multiple smaller beads onto each of the wires, to form the legs. Use the pliers to bend the end of each wire, then form a loop and cut off the excess. **3. Suspend** a bead from each of these loops for the feet. **4. To make** the arms, take approximately 4 inches of wire and bend it in two. Wrap it tightly between the top two beads (head bead and body bead), then string the beads onto each arm, finishing with one smaller bead. Use the pliers to bend the ends of the wires over the final smaller beads. **5. Finish** by attaching the little man to the keyring chain using the loop on the top of his head.

Forest Feathers Lucky Charm

YOU WILL NEED:

- flat suede lace
- leather laces
- thin satin and organza ribbons
- thin strips of fancy wool
- a few pieces of green felt
- scissors
- green thread
- a needle

- a wooden bead (25 mm in diameter)
- green and brown cabled cotton (number 5) for crocheting
- a number 2 crochet needle
- fancy green-hued glass beads
- polished mother-of-pearl pieces
- little feathers

1. **Gather** together the suede lace, the leather laces (leave a few out), the ribbons, and the wool strips, and fold them in half. (The ribbons and other elements should each be about 10 inches long.) Fix this set of materials together by tying and knotting one of the leather laces around the bunch a short distance from the top. Form a kind of tassel by winding another length of leather around this bunch and knot it firmly to secure it. 2. **Cut** out leaf shapes from the felt. Use long stitches to make veins on the leaves. 3. **Cover** the wooden bead with crochet (*see p. 296*). 4. **Decorate** the various laces and ribbons by stringing them with beads, mother-of-pearl, leaves, feathers, and the crocheted bead, keeping them in place using knots tied at various levels. 5. **Adjust** the lengths by trimming them with the scissors. Use a leather lace to hang the lucky charm from your bag.

Fancy Felted Key Ring

YOU WILL NEED:

- a pencil
- yellow wool felt
- scissors
- a needle
- beading wire
- 3 pink felted balls (1–1½ inches in diameter)
- pink seed beads
- a crimp bead
- a key ring
- flat-nose pliers
- wire cutters

1. Trace and cut out the flower pattern (*see p. 309*) six times on the yellow wool felt. **2. Thread** the beading wire onto the needle and string a felt ball, 6 seed beads, 2 felt flowers, and 6 seed beads onto the wire in that order. Repeat that pattern two more times on the same length of wire. **3. Finish** by stringing on about 3 inches of seed beads. Add a crimp bead after the last seed bead. Pass the wire through the key ring, back through the crimp bead, and through about an inch worth of the seed beads. Using the flat-nose pliers, crimp the crimp bead tightly and trim any excess wire.

Lucky Charm

YOU WILL NEED:

- iron
- a 2½ inch square of thick fabric
- nylon thread
- 7 navy blue buttons (½ inch in diameter)
- white and navy-blue cotton thread
- a navy-blue button (¾ inch in diameter)
- black, green, and pearly-white seed beads
- scissors
- a needle
- small crimp beads
- flat-nose pliers
- a clasp (springring, lobster, or box)
- a 2¼ inch square of black felt
- fabric glue

1. Use the iron and press to make a hem ⅓ of an inch wide around the edge of the square of fabric and secure the hem using a few tack stitches. Sew the small buttons onto the center of the square of fabric using the navy-blue thread, placing them in a circle. **2. Now** sew the large button into the center of the circle. Sew the pearly-white seed beads around the button flower, using the white cotton thread. **3. Cut** a 20½ inch length of nylon thread and use the needle to thread it into the hem underneath the square of fabric. Center the square on the nylon thread and string black and green seed beads onto it, creating patterns of color. String one crimp bead onto each end of the nylon thread and pass the thread back through the crimp beads. **4. Crimp** the beads firmly with the flat-nose pliers, leaving the excess nylon threads to form two small loops. Attach the clasp to these loops. Use the fabric glue to attach the black felt square to the back of the square of fabric.

Spring Flower

YOU WILL NEED:

- white felt
- a soft pencil
- scissors
- white cotton thread
- a needle
- small pearly-white buttons
- beading wire (approx. 12 inches total)
- wire cutters
- seed beads in various colors
- small crimp beads
- flat-nose pliers
- fabric glue
- a 1¼-inch-long safety-pin base

1. Draw a flower shape (approximately 3½ inches across) on the white felt with the soft pencil. Place a second piece of felt underneath and cut both of the felt flower shapes out with the scissors. **2. Cover** one of the felt flowers entirely with buttons (by sewing them on). **3. Use** the tip of the scissors to make two small holes in the center of the flower. Cut three pieces of beading wire, each one measuring about 4 inches long. Pass the threads through the first hole in the flower and back out through the second. String the seed beads onto these threads, placing and crimping a crimp bead on each end to hold the seed beads in place. **4. Apply** the fabric glue to the back of the buttoned flower and stick the second felt flower to the back of it. Leave it to dry, then sew the safety-pin base onto the back of the flower.

PART TWO

Crafts for Your Home

Bookmark

YOU WILL NEED:

- a 36-inch glittery orange loopie cord (tubular, hollow plastic lace)
- scissors
- metal wire
- wire cutters

1. Cut a 16-inch length from the cord and insert 11 inches of metal wire into it. **2. Take** the bottom 2⅓ inches of the end of the cord into which you inserted the metal wire and roll it into a spiral. **3. Take** the rest of the cord (20 inches) and start a four-thread round boondoggle (*see p. 297*), with the first length of cord placed in the middle of it, make three stitches and cut off the excess cord. **4. Repeat** this operation 1½ inches further on, and again 1½ inches above that.

Butterfly Card

YOU WILL NEED:

- an 11 x 17-inch sheet of light-pink card stock
- ruler
- a pencil and eraser
- utility knife and cutting mat
- an 8½ x 11-inch sheet of lined white tracing paper
- decorative scissors
- an 8½ x 11-inch sheet of pink paper
- glue stick
- a decorative butterfly mounted on a stem
- wire cutters
- a needle

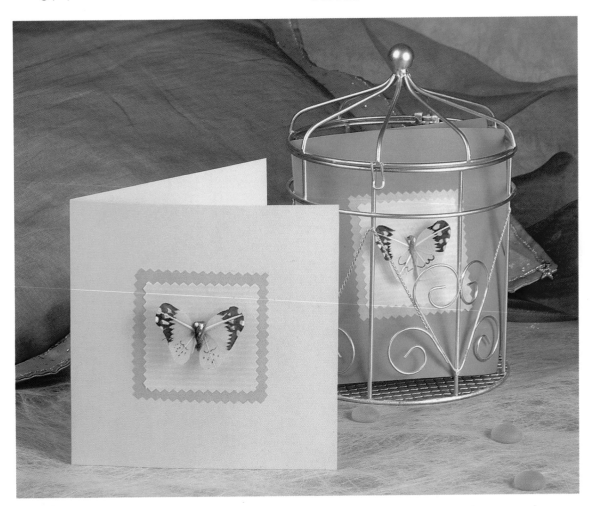

1. **Draw** a rectangle measuring 12¼ x 6 inches on the light-pink card. Cut it out using the utility knife and fold it in half to form a near square. Draw a 6-inch square on the tracing paper and cut it out using the decorative scissors. Slip it inside the card intended for your message. 2. **Cut** out a 3-inch square from the pink paper using the decorative scissors. Glue it to the front center of the card. 3. **Cut** out a 2½-inch square from the tracing paper using the decorative scissors. Glue it on top of the little pink square. 4. **With** the wire cutters, cut the stem of the butterfly down to 1⅓ inches. Prick a hole in the center of the card with the needle and stick the stem of the butterfly through the hole, folding down the end on the other side.

Organdy Overlay Card

YOU WILL NEED:

- a sheet of cream-colored, textured 11 x 17-inch card stock
- a ruler
- a pencil and eraser
- a utility knife and cutting mat
- a sheet of honey-colored 8½ x 11-inch lined tracing paper

- organdy cloth scraps in three colors
- cream-colored thread
- a needle
- scissors
- 12 seed beads
- a fine-tipped permanent silver marker pen

1. Fold the cream-colored card in half and trace a 6-inch square on it. The first side should be along the fold. Cut out the square with the utility knife, leaving the folded side intact. Erase any remaining pencil marks. Fold the sheet of lined tracing paper in two and trim it to make it the same size as the card. **2. Cut** out three squares of organdy measuring 2⅓ inches, 4 inches, and 5 inches square. Unravel a bit of the edges of the two largest squares. **3. Place** the squares on top of each other on the card, starting with the largest and finishing with the smallest. Sew a bead into the corner of each square of organdy, through the card, cutting off the thread inside. **4. Write** the word "invitation" on the sheet of tracing paper with the silver pen. Slip the folded sheet of tracing paper into the card.

Heartfelt Package

YOU WILL NEED:

- a pebble
- a small paintbrush
- acrylic paint: red, dark red, gold
- red craft paper
- red ribbon
- glue

1. Paint the pebble dark red. Leave it to dry. **2. Paint** a red heart in the middle of it (*see p. 308*). Leave it to dry. **3. Draw** the outline of a gold heart on the pebble, but shifted slightly off-center from the red heart (see photo). Leave it to dry. **4. Wrap** up your gift in the red craft paper. Cut two 8-inch lengths of tying ribbon, trimming the ends into points. Glue them onto the package as in the photo. Glue the pebble on top.

Surprise Scrapbook

YOU WILL NEED:

- 4 paper grocery bags with gussets
- a 3-hole paper punch
- 3 large hole reinforcers
- bits of ribbon
- spray adhesive
- sheets of paper with printed designs, personal photographs, paper flowers, and other decorations

1. Fold the paper bags in two and place them inside each other head to foot. Use the hole puncher to make three large holes and place a hole reinforcer over each of them. Thread the ribbon through the holes and knot it at the end. **2. Using** spray adhesive, stick on the cutouts from the printed paper and add all of the decorations and any photos you like. What is unusual about this scrapbook is the way in which one can hide pages and treasures in the gussets — you can do whatever you like inside the paper bag openings. *A word of warning*: brown paper, such as that used to make grocery bags, is acidic and can damage photos. So stick your photos on nonacidic paper and then attach to the brown paper, or use photocopies (color or hand-colored black and white) of your photographs.

Elegant Homemade Menu

YOU WILL NEED:

- a sheet of blue iridescent card stock (8½ x 11 inches)
- a ruler
- a pencil and eraser
- utility knife and cutting mat
- 2 sheets of ivory-colored iridescent paper (8½ x 11 inches)
- spray adhesive
- scissors
- a drawing compass
- removable sticky tape
- sewing machine

1. Fold the blue card in half and cut off a 2-inch strip to shorten the rectangle so that it measures 4¼ x 9 inches. On the ivory-colored paper draw a rectangle measuring 4¼ x 9 inches and cut it out — you will later write out the menu on this sheet and slip it inside the card. **2. Take** the rest of the sheet of ivory paper and tear off a strip 10 inches long, then cut it to a width of 2¾ inches (you should end up with a rectangle that has one long torn side). Spray this piece with adhesive and place it vertically on the card (with the torn side facing toward the center) so that it covers a little more than half of the surface. Trim any excess edges. **3. Mark** out a 1½-inch-square on the inside of the cover of the card. This square should be centered left to right and 2 inches from the top of the card. Cut out this square to make a window. **4. Using** the drawing compass, trace a 1½-inch-diameter circle from a scrap of the ivory paper. Cut the circle out carefully. Fix a strip of removable sticky tape behind the window inside the card. Position the disc in the center of the opening on the sticky tape. **5. Trace** a line vertically down the center of the first page (the menu cover) with a pencil. Use the sewing machine to stitch all the way along this pencil line. Cut off the excess thread and remove the sticky tape.

Best Friend Collage

YOU WILL NEED:

- a sheet of paper printed with circle motifs (11 x 17 inches)
- scissors
- glue
- a sheet of plain white paper (11 x 17 inches)

- a sheet of medium-blue paper (8½ x 11 inches)
- a square photo
- self-adhesive letters and numbers
- 6 ribbons of different colors and patterns
- a stapler and staples

1. Cut a 2⅓ x 11¾-inch rectangle from the sheet of circle-motif paper and glue it onto the top of the sheet of plain white paper. Cut out a 6-inch square from the medium-blue paper. Glue the photo on the sheet of white paper, with the blue square next to it. **2. Cut** a half circle from the circle-motif paper. Place self-adhesive numbers on it to make the date and glue it alongside the photo. **3. Stretch** the ribbons diagonally across the page so that they cross each other and staple them in place. Cut out the circle tag (*see p. 307*), write a simple photo caption on it with the self-adhesive letters, and tie it to a ribbon to attach it to the collage.

Valentine Card

YOU WILL NEED:

- a sheet of deep-red card stock (11 x 17 inches)
- a sheet of ivory-colored tracing paper (11 x 17 inches)
- a pencil with eraser
- a ruler
- a utility knife and cutting mat
- a sheet of red iridescent paper (8½ x 11 inches)
- spray adhesive
- leopard-skin design fake fur
- a pin
- pinking shears
- double-sided sticky tape

1. **Fold** the red card in half and trace a 6-inch square on it using the folded side as the first edge. Do the same with the tracing paper. Cut out the shapes using the utility knife. Erase any remaining pencil traces. Slip the folded sheet of tracing paper into the folded card. **2. Trace** a 5½-inch square on the sheet of red iridescent paper. Cut it out and stick it onto the front of the card using the spray adhesive. **3. Draw** a heart motif (like the one in the photo) on a sheet of scrap paper. Pin it to the back of the piece of fake fur and use the pinking shears to cut out the heart shape. Use small pieces of double-sided sticky tape to attach the heart to the center of the card. Write your message on the inside tracing paper.

Little Flower Card

YOU WILL NEED

- a sheet of pink card stock (11 x 17 inches)
- ruler
- a pencil with eraser
- utility knife and cutting mat
- a sheet of lime-green card stock (11 x 17 inches)
- a piece of pink burlap
  (at least 5 inches square)
- wide double-sided sticky tape with strong
  adhesive properties
- white fluted card stock (8½ x 11 inches)
- scissors
- strong glue in a tube or a glue gun
- a small fabric flower
- a hole puncher
- light-pink ribbon (⅓ inch wide)

1. **Fold** the sheet of pink paper in two and trace a 6-inch square on it. Use the folded edge as the first side. Use the utility knife to cut out the square. Erase any remaining pencil marks. Do the same with the line-green paper. 2. **Cut** out a 5-inch square of burlap. Use a piece of double-sided tape in the center to fix it to the center of the pink card. 3. **Use** the scissors to cut out a 3¼-inch square from the white fluted card. Use another piece of double-sided tape to fix it to the center of the burlap square (covering the first piece of tape). 4. **Glue** the small fabric flower to the center of the white square, using a drop of strong glue. 5. **Slip** the folded sheet of lime-green card inside the folded sheet of pink card and punch a hole in the center of the right-hand edge. Attach the ribbon and tie a pretty bow.

Quilted Book Cover

YOU WILL NEED:

- paper napkins with designs
- scissors
- a sheet of thick paper
- adhesive varnish
- a spiral-bound notebook
- a sheet of paper as big as the notebook cover
- scraps of printed paper
- a photocopy of a photo made on pink paper
- 4 photo corners
- a sewing kit or a sewing machine
- a round-headed paper fastener (the kind with two prongs)

1. Use the scissors to cut out interesting designs from the paper napkins, but keep only the printed layer and glue it onto the thick paper with the adhesive varnish. **2. Glue** the pieces of printed paper, the photo, and the photo corners onto a sheet of paper the same size as the notebook and sew around their edges either by hand or with a sewing machine. Cut out a shape you like from the printed paper and attach it using the paper fastener. **3. Glue** the completed decorative page onto the front of the notebook using adhesive varnish.

Photo Collage

YOU WILL NEED:

- a (4 x 6-inch) photo (vertical format)
- a (4 x 6-inch) photo (horizontal format)
- 2 sheets of deep-purple paper (11 x 17 inches)
- glue
- a hole puncher
- 2 sheets of sand-colored paper (12 inches square)
- a sheet of lavender-colored paper (12 inches long)
- a sheet of paper printed with a topographical map
- 2 metal photo corners
- a ruler
- 3 small photos
- a label holder (*see pattern on p. 309*)
- 2 paper fasteners
- bits of string
- transparent ink
- transparent embossing powder
- embossing gun
- a small safety pin

To make the large collage: 1. Glue the 2 larger photos onto deep-purple paper rectangles (4¼ x 6¼ inches). Use the hole punch to make decorative holes in one of the paper frames. Glue the paper framed photos to a sheet of sand-colored paper. **2. Cut** a few 12-inch horizontal strips of paper from the remaining papers and glue them in places as horizontal stripes between the two photos. **3. Tear** the map paper down one edge and place it so that it covers one-third of the width of the sand-colored paper, possibly covering a portion of one of the photos. **4. Glue** the two photo corners to the bottom on the lower photo.

To make the little book: 1. Fold a piece of sand-colored paper (5⅓ x 2⅓ inches) into three equal parts and round off the corners with the hole puncher. **2. Measure** the dimensions of each section, reduce by a small fraction on each side, and cut three pieces of the deep-purple paper to fit the trifold book. Use the hole punch to make decorative holes in the paper frames. Glue the paper inside the little book, then glue your 3 small photos on top of each section. **3. Cut** out the label holder (*see p. 309*) and use two paper fasteners to attach it to the cover. Knot the bits of string to one of the paper fasteners. **4. Cut** out a circle from the map paper. Ink this paper circle with the transparent ink, sprinkle it with transparent embossing powder, and heat with the embossing gun: it will form a kind of varnish layer. Attach the circle to the bits of string using a small safety pin.

When I Was Young

YOU WILL NEED:

- scraps of printed paper
- a photo (4 x 6 inches)
- a stapler and colored staples
- bits of string
- eyelets
- a sheet of colored paper (6½ x 5⅓ inches)
- glue
- a wooden craft stick
- a round label made of tracing paper
- a foam stamp to make decorative shapes
- white acrylic paint
- a sheet of plain pink paper (12 inches square)
- burlap
- black ink
- self-adhesive letters
- paper fasteners
- a fabric flower
- a ribbon
- a hammer
- a bottle top
- beads
- a postage-stamp hole puncher
- white transparent embossing powder
- a decorative hole puncher

1. **Start** with the frame. Cut out strips of printed paper ⅓ of an inch wide and place them around the photo. Attach them to each other with staples and by passing bits of string through eyelets. Glue the photo onto a larger rectangle of paper measuring 6½ x 5⅓ inches. 2. **Glue** the craft stick to the bottom of the photo frame. Use an eyelet to attach the round label to the frame. 3. **Using** the decorative stamp and the white acrylic paint, decorate the edges of the 12-inch sheet of pink paper. Staple a strip of burlap across the pink paper, just below its center. Glue the framed photo to the pink paper, roughly lining the bottom of the photo frame with the bottom edge of the burlap. 4. **Write** your childhood memory by hand on a piece of printed paper, except for a few words stamped in black ink and written with self-adhesive letters. Glue the piece of paper with the text on it to another piece of printed paper. 5. **To make** the first name, cut out a large initial from the plain paper and a second larger initial from the printed paper and stick one onto the other. Attach a fabric flower with a paper fastener, knot bits of string, and staple a ribbon to it. 6. **Use** a hammer to flatten the bottle top, then stick on a self-adhesive letter of your choice. Use strong glue to stick beads onto one of the letters. Use the postage-stamp hole puncher to create postage-stamp shapes. The letter "E" in the photo was stamped in black ink, then embossed with transparent powder. The letter "A" was cut out from a magazine, then embossed in the same way, before a shape cut using the decorative hole puncher was glued on top of it. Finish by personalizing your first name!

Savory Invitation

YOU WILL NEED:

- brown card stock printed with a texture pattern (20 x 25½ inches)
- a straightedge ruler
- a pencil with eraser
- a utility knife and cutting mat
- double-sided sticky tape (transparent)
- pink burlap

- scissors
- a sheet of red tracing paper (8½ x 11 inches)
- 2 dried bay leaves
- a gold fine-tipped felt pen

1. Trace out a rectangle measuring 21¼ inches wide x 7 inches high on the brown card. Using the utility knife and the straightedge ruler, cut out the long rectangle. Trace vertical lines to divide the width into three even squares. Fold the left-hand flap toward the inside and down on top of the central square. Trace a 4⅓-inch square on the center of the left-hand flap and, while keeping the left-hand flap pressed down firmly on the center square, cut out the window shape from both squares of card. Attach strips of double-sided sticky tape around the window in the central square. **2. Cut** out a 5-inch square of pink burlap and press it down onto the double-sided sticky tape. Now attach strips of double-sided sticky tape around the edges of the central square and close the front flap down onto it so that the two squares are stuck together. **3. Cut** out a 7-inch square from the sheet of red tracing paper. Place the bay leaves head to toe in the middle of this sheet in line with the diagonal and keeping a little gap between them. Fix them in place using small pieces of double-sided sticky tape. Write the word "invitation" between the two leaves with the gold felt pen.

Secret Diary

YOU WILL NEED:

- a pebble
- acrylic paint: light-brown, white
- a small paintbrush
- a notebook bound with a textured paper
- glue
- 16 inches of twine

1. Paint the top of the pebble brown. Leave it to dry. **2. Paint** a white keyhole on it. Leave it to dry. **3. Glue** the pebble to the cover of the notebook. Leave it to dry. **4. Wrap** the twine around the book a few times and once around the "lock."

Leaf Note

YOU WILL NEED:

- a sheet of mauve paper printed with a texture effect (8½ x 11 inches)
- a pencil with eraser
- a ruler
- a utility knife and cutting mat
- a decorative tree leaf
- spray adhesive
- a sheet of white drawing paper (8½ x 11 inches)
- a sheet of tracing paper (8½ x 11 inches)
- scissors
- plum-colored raffia
- a silver permanent felt-tip pen

1. Trace out a 5½-inch square on the mauve paper and cut it out. Spray the decorative tree leaf with adhesive and place it diagonally on the square of mauve paper. **2. Trace** out a 6¼-inch square on the sheet of white drawing paper and tear down the four sides of the square along the lines you have traced. Erase any pencil marks left on this ripped-edge square of white drawing paper. Do the same thing with the tracing paper, but make the square just under 6¾ inches on a side. **3. Glue** the mauve square onto the white square and then glue that onto the square of tracing paper. **4. Use** the scissors or utility knife to make two little holes in a top corner. Pass a piece of raffia through these holes and tie a little bow. Write your message on the back in silver felt-tip pen.

Notebook Cover

YOU WILL NEED:

- a notebook
- felt: turquoise, brown
- a pencil
- scissors

- fabric glue
- brown lace
- a decorative pen

1. Place the notebook on the turquoise felt, open it, and trace out the shape of its cover, but with an extra ⅓ of an inch around the edges. **2. To** make the pen loops, make two slits in the felt 1½ inches from the edge, spacing the slits ¾ of an inch apart. Make two such pairs of slits, one toward the top of the cover and one toward the bottom. Cut two strips of brown felt 2 inches long by ⅔ of an inch wide. Pass these through the slits to form the pen loops. Glue inside. **3. Glue** the turquoise felt onto the notebook, taking care to glue the excess edges inside the cover. **4. Cut** out two pieces of brown felt that are ⅓ of an inch smaller than the inside of the cover. Glue one piece inside the front cover and the other piece inside the back cover. **5. Glue** one strip of lace along the bottom of the notebook cover (front and back sides). **6. Cut** out small shapes from the turquoise felt and glue them onto the strip of lace, spaced well apart. Leave to dry. **7. Slip** the pen through the brown loops.

CD Book

YOU WILL NEED:

- paper CD pockets
- a hole puncher
- hole reinforcers
- 2 metal binder rings
- plain and printed sheets of paper
- personal photos
- glue
- transfer and sticker letters

1. Punch two holes along the left edge of the CD pockets. Place the hole reinforcers over the holes (front and back sides) so that they do not get any wider. Link the pockets together with the binder rings. **2. To** make the cover: Measure the exact dimensions of your CD pockets and cut squares of the same size from the various printed papers. Choose one paper square or combine several pieces and glue them to the front CD pocket. Using the CD window as a template, trim a personal photo to the same circular shape. Glue this photo into place. Use the transfer and sticker letters to write your CD book's title on this cover. **3. For** the other pages, use the square dimensions from above to crop the photo so that it fits into the CD pocket with your subject centered in the round window. Cut out more squares from the printed paper to be glued onto the remaining pockets. Decorate all printed pockets with your personal photos and paper.

Chopstick Rests

YOU WILL NEED:

- 2 oval pebbles
- acrylic paint: black, red, gold
- a paintbrush
- a sponge

1. Paint the pebbles black. Leave them to dry. **2. Use** the sponge to dab a few spots of gold paint onto a pebble to mimic leaves. Leave it to dry. **3. Paint** the cherry tree branch red (*see p. 307*). Leave it to dry. **4. Paint** the other pebble in reverse: Dab spots of red paint onto it with the sponge and then paint the branch in gold. Let both rocks dry completely before using.

Bright & Shiny Napkin Rings

YOU WILL NEED:

- 16 small pebbles
- white acrylic paint
- a paintbrush
- sky-blue relief paint (in a tube)
- 4 napkin rings decorated with a mosaic of mirrors
- glue

1. Paint the top and sides of the pebbles white. Leave them to dry. **2. Paint** triangles on the pebbles using the relief paint directly from the tube, imitating the shapes of the mosaic pieces. Leave them to dry. **3. Glue** 4 pebbles onto each of the 4 napkin rings. Leave to dry.

Cocktail Sticks

YOU WILL NEED:

- 4 loopie cords (tubular, hollow plastic lace):
  1 yellow, 1 blue, 1 red, 1 purple
- 4 flower-shaped (2-hole) buttons:
  1 yellow, 1 blue, 1 red, 1 purple
- 4 plastic cocktail sticks:
  1 green, 1 blue, 1 yellow, 1 pink

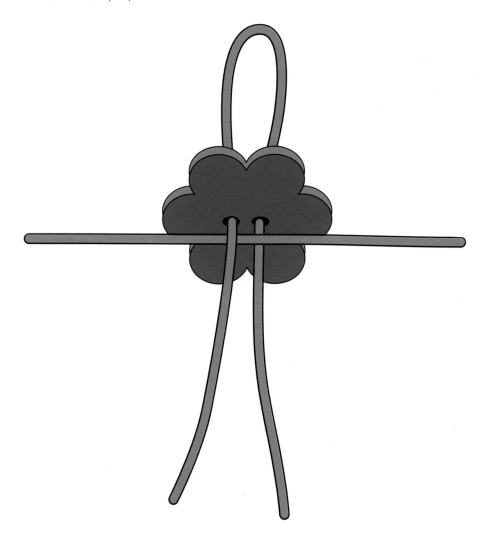

1. Cut one of the loopie cords in half. **2. Take** one of the halved loopie cords and pass the two ends through the holes of one of the buttons. **3. Slip** the second halved loopie cord underneath the button and make an initial stitch with the two pieces. **4. Place** a cocktail stick in the center and braid a round four-thread boondoggle (*see pp. 297 to 298*) 1¼ inches long. **5. Tighten** well and cut off any excess. **6. Proceed** in the same way for the three other sticks.

Iris

YOU WILL NEED:

- a cloth napkin (ironed and perhaps starched, to hold final shape better)

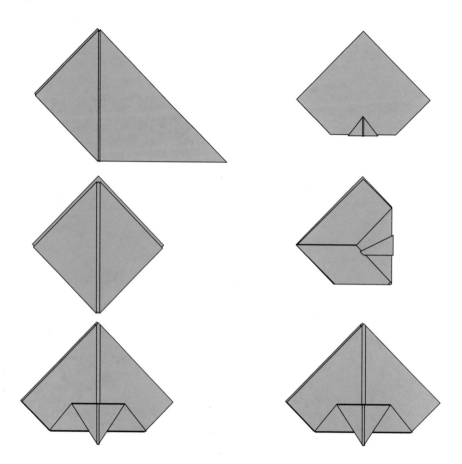

1. **Place** the napkin down flat, with the stitched turned-up side facing up. 2. **Fold** the napkin in two along the diagonal, then turn the resulting triangle shape so that the longest edge runs along the bottom and the point is at the top. 3. **Fold** the lower corners onto the upper point to form a square. 4. **Fold** the lower point up to the center, then fold it back on itself toward the bottom so that it sticks over the edge by ¾ of an inch. 5. **Fold** this point underneath the napkin. 6. **Turn** over the napkin. 7. **Fold** the sides into the center and insert one inside the other. 8. **Stand** the napkin upright and fold the points of the two side pieces downward to create the flower shape.

Tablecloth Weights

YOU WILL NEED:

- 4 pebbles of approximately equal size and weight
- acrylic paint: orange, yellow, turquoise, dark red
- a paintbrush
- glossy acrylic varnish in spray can
- four curtain rings with spring clips

1. Paint the pebbles completely orange. Leave them to dry. **2. Paint** a turquoise circle in the center of each pebble top, a smaller yellow circle next to the turquoise one, and dark red circle off to one side. Leave the pebbles to dry. **3. Spray** each pebble with a layer of glossy varnish. Leave them to dry. **4. Glue** the spring clips to the back of the pebbles. Leave them to dry. Attach to the four corners of your tablecloth to keep the cloth from blowing or sliding from the table.

Tea Cozy

YOU WILL NEED:

- felt: turquoise, yellow, orange, red
- thread: turquoise, yellow, red
- sewing machine
- yellow-colored pearl cotton thread
- a brown felt-tip pen (for fabric)
- scissors
- a needle
- red seed beads

1. Enlarge the stencil A (*see p. 305*) 150% and trace on the turquoise felt folded in two, then cut it out, leaving an excess ⅓ inch around the edge. **2. Trace** stencils B and C (*p. 305*) on the yellow felt folded in two and cut it out. **3. Trace** stencil D (*p. 305*) on the red felt and cut it out. Cut out 30 thin strips of the orange felt (⅓ inch long) for the flowers. **4. Place** the yellow pieces (B and C) on the turquoise felt as indicated on the pattern and machine stitch them. **5. Embroider** the hooves with a running stitch, using the yellow pearl cotton thread. For the flowers, stitch three strips of orange felt together in the center to form one flower. Sew the flower onto the yellow strip. Sew one red seed bead in the middle of the flower. Repeat for the rest of the flowers. **6. Trace** out the elephant's ears, trunk, and eyes using the brown felt-tip pen. Place the two pieces of turquoise felt right sides together. Slip the strip of yellow felt (¾ inch x 4 inches) inside at the top, leaving an excess of ⅓ of an inch. Machine stitch it in place. Turn inside out. **7. Use** tack stitches to attach the red kerchief onto the elephant's head, then embroider it with a few seed beads.

Painted Star Bowl

YOU WILL NEED:

- earthenware bowl and a stand
- red acrylic paint
- a paintbrush
- paper with star motifs
- adhesive varnish
- scissors

1. Paint the inside of the bowl red. Leave it to dry, then turn it over and paint the outside. Leave it to dry and then give it a second coat of paint in the same manner. **2. Carefully** cut out the stars — several small ones for the outside and inside, and a larger one to place in the center of the bowl. **3. Proceed** by zones: lay down a coat of adhesive varnish and place the stars on top. Continue in this manner until you have placed all the stars and applied a base coat over the entire surface. Then lay down another coat of varnish over the whole surface to avoid differences in shininess. Leave it to dry.

Thimble Trivet

YOU WILL NEED:

- thin cardboard
- a ruler
- scissors
- a sheet of rubber (⅛ to ¼ inch thick), or a soft-sided mouse pad
- a utility knife and cutting mat
- a piece of board (no smaller than 8 x 8 inches)
- double-sided sticky tape
- a punch tool (⅔ inch in diameter) (such as a leather hole punch)
- a hammer
- a black marker pen
- 49 thimbles
- cyanoacrylate glue (e.g. Super Glue or Krazy Glue)

1. Cut a piece from the cardboard measuring 6½ inches square. Trace a border inside the four sides of the square, ⅔ of an inch from the edge, then mark out grid lines every ¾ of an inch to make a template. Cut the piece of rubber to the same exterior dimensions as the cardboard. **2. Place** the rubber on top of the piece of board and the cardboard template on top of that. Fix a little of the double-sided sticky tape to the underside of the cardboard and attach it to the rubber. Place the punch at the intersections of the gridlines marked on the template and strike it with the hammer. You should end up with a square pattern of seven holes by seven holes. **3. Use** the marker pen to mark out round corners on the piece of rubber — you might want to use a small round container cover as a guide. Cut these corners with the scissors. **4. Insert** a thimble in each hole, having placed a little glue around the base of each one to hold it in place.

Slimming Diet Napkin Rings

YOU WILL NEED:

- several tape measures
- a ruler
- scissors or a utility knife and cutting mat
- self-adhesive plastic film
- cyanoacrylate glue (e.g. Super Glue or Krazy Glue)
- sewing machine
- rivets and rivet pliers

1. To make one napkin ring: Measure the width of the tape measures when placed side by side (approximately 2 inches). Cut out a rectangle of plastic film measuring 6¼ inches long by the width of your combined tape measures. Remove the protective covering from the plastic film's adhesive strip. **2. Glue** the tape measures onto the plastic film, touching side by side. Cut off any excess film. **3. Use** the sewing machine to straight-stitch around the edges of the tape measure rectangle you've created. Make a knot when you reach the end, and cover this with a spot of glue. Leave it to dry. **4. Join** the two ends of the rectangle to form a napkin ring and fix in place with two rivets. The pliers you will need to do this are usually sold with the rivets. **5. Repeat** entire process for as many napkin rings as you desire.

Star

YOU WILL NEED:

● a cloth napkin (ironed and perhaps starched)

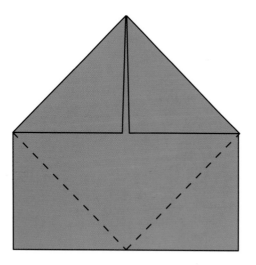 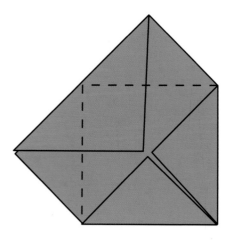

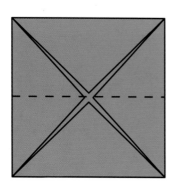 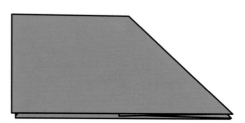

1. Place the napkin down flat, with the stitched turned-up side facing up. **2. Fold** the four corners in toward the center. **3. Fold** the four new corners toward the center. **4. Fold** the napkin in half, from top to bottom. **5. Fold** the right-side top edge inside. This folded edge will now be a vertical fold and it will form two triangular flaps to the outside right corner. Make the same fold with the left top edge. **6. Stand** up and shape.

Checkmate Table

YOU WILL NEED:

- 16 blue bottle tops
- 16 white bottle tops
- a drill and drill bits
- hooks, screws, eyelets, hinge pins, nuts, washers, etc., to form the chess pieces (make sure you have matching pieces for 2 kings, 2 queens, 4 rooks, 4 bishops, 4 knights, and 16 pawns)
- a glue gun and glue sticks
- sheets of contact paper
- a ruler
- scissors
- a Formica table
- newspaper and making tape
- silver spray paint

1. Drill holes in the bottle tops that are the same size as the metal pieces you will be fitting into them. Push the corresponding metal piece firmly into the hole. **2. Use** the glue gun to fix the metal pieces in place from underneath. **3. Cut** out 32 squares (1⅓ inches each) from the contact paper. Make a chessboard centered in the middle of the table. **4. Cover** the top of the table with newspaper and masking tape, leaving the square area of the chessboard unprotected. Spray paint the chessboard portion of the table with the silver paint. Leave it to dry. **5. Remove** the newspaper from the outer edges of the table top. Remove the adhesive squares with the tip of a knife to reveal your tabletop chessboard. Place the chess pieces on the board.

Waiting for Spring

YOU WILL NEED:

- enough light-colored pebbles of medium size to fill your vase
- acrylic paint: spring-green, red, black
- a small paintbrush
- a small pebble
- a clear glass vase
- a large artificial flower
- wire cutters

1. Use the spring-green paint to paint leaves, twigs, and plant shapes on both sides of the medium-sized pebbles. Leave them to dry. **2. Paint** a red and black ladybug on the small pebble. Leave it to dry. **3. Place** the pebbles in the vase and add the flower, shortening its stem with the wire cutters if necessary. **4. Place** the ladybug pebble wherever you wish: on the flower, in the vase, near the vase.

Pumpkin Tray

YOU WILL NEED:

- paper with pumpkin carriage (3) and star motifs (several)
- scissors
- a pink plastic tray
- adhesive varnish
- a flat paintbrush

1. Carefully cut out the pumpkin carriages and the stars. **2. Cover** the center of the tray with adhesive varnish, place the first carriage right in the middle, and cover it with adhesive varnish. **3. Cover** the sides with adhesive varnish, place the two other carriages on the tray, and cover them with adhesive varnish. **4. Brush** a coat of adhesive varnish around the top edges of the carriages, place the stars, and cover them with adhesive varnish. Leave to dry. **5. Lay** a final coat of adhesive varnish over the whole tray and leave to dry.

Roll

YOU WILL NEED:

- a cloth napkin (ironed and perhaps starched)

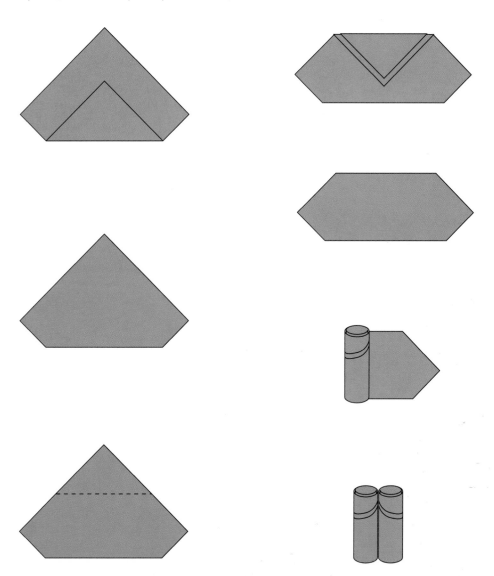

This folding technique works best with a napkin with a top and bottom side of two different colors.
1. Place the napkin down flat, with the stitched turned-up side facing up. **2. Fold** the napkin in two diagonally, positioning the lower point 2 inches below the upper point. **3. Turn** over the napkin. **4. Fold** over the two points until they are ¼ of an inch from the base. **5. Turn** over the napkin. **6. Roll** the left- and right-hand points together until they meet in the center. **7. Turn** over the napkin and shape it as required.

Crazy Cups

YOU WILL NEED:

- plastic funnels of different sizes and colors
- a glue gun and glue sticks

1. Fit pairs of funnels together by inserting the long ends into each other. **2. Pour** glue from the glue gun into the bottom of the funnels to seal them. Leave the glue to harden. Pour more glue into the funnel to make a flat bottom.

Rock Solid Candleholder

YOU WILL NEED:

- white air-dry modeling clay
- 8 to 10 pebbles
- metallic orange acrylic paint
- a paintbrush
- glue
- a clear ground glass candle jar
- an orange perfumed candle

1. Flatten the white clay to a thickness of ¼ of an inch. Cut out a 6-inch diameter disk. Leave it to dry for 24 hours. **2. Paint** the pebbles and the disk metallic orange. Leave them to dry. **3. Place** the pebbles around the edge of the disk and test their stability and how well they fit onto each other. Lightly scratch away the paint on the surface of the pebble that will rest on the clay disk so that the glue will stick better. **4. Glue** the pebbles onto the disk and also to each other if possible. Leave to dry. **5. Paint** a strip of metallic orange around the top of the candle jar and leave it to dry. **6. Place** the candle in the jar and the jar on its base.

Strawberry Tart Platter

YOU WILL NEED:

- paper with strawberry designs
- scissors
- a glass tart platter with footed base

- adhesive varnish
- a flat brush
- spray acrylic or polyurethane (as sealant)

1. Carefully cut the strawberry designs from the paper. **2. Turn** the platter upside down with the footed base in the air. Use the flat brush to apply a coat of adhesive varnish to the underside of the platter. Place a number of strawberry pictures on the underside of the platter. Cover with adhesive varnish. Leave to dry. **3. Apply** a second coat of adhesive varnish for evenness. Repeat the process for the underside of the footed base. **4. Coat** the undersides of the platter and the footed base with the acrylic or polyurethane sealant: Spray several coats of the sealant; make sure to let it dry completely between each coat. Once it is sealed, you will be able to wash the platter carefully by hand.

Salad Servers

YOU WILL NEED:

- 8 loopie cords (tubular, hollow plastic lace): 4 green transparent, 4 blue transparent
- 2 salad servers
- scissors

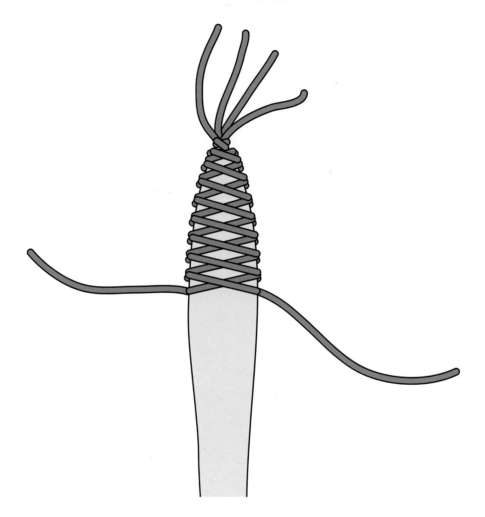

1. Knot the four blue cords together 1¼ inches from their ends. **2. Make** an initial stitch. **3. Slip** the handle of a salad server into the center and braid a square boondoggle (*see p. 296*). **4. Braid** approximately 3½ inches, knot the cords together in pairs, and cut off the excess. Repeat for the other salad server, using the green cords.

Flora Place Mats

YOU WILL NEED:

- paper with leaf and flower designs
- scissors
- two blue raffia place mats
- adhesive varnish
- a flat paintbrush

1. Carefully cut out all of the flower and the leaf designs. **2. Apply** a coat of adhesive varnish to the areas on the place mats where you wish to place the designs, including an excess area of ¼ of an inch. Place the paper cutouts on these areas. **3. Apply** a coat of adhesive varnish over the composition, again including an excess area of ¼ of an inch. Leave to dry. **4. Apply** a second coat of adhesive varnish and let it dry.

Napkin Rings

YOU WILL NEED:

- wooden napkin rings
- purple acrylic paint
- a flat paintbrush
- thin paper printed with mostly pink designs
- adhesive varnish
- scissors

1. **Paint** the inside of the napkin rings purple. Leave them to dry. 2. **Tear** the paper into pieces. Cover part of each napkin ring with adhesive varnish. Place the pieces of paper on top. Continue to cover the entire outside of the napkin ring in this way, overlapping the pieces of paper. Lay a thin coat of adhesive varnish over the pieces of paper. Leave the fully papered napkin rings to dry. 3. **Trim** any excess paper that might protrude over the edges.

Bud

YOU WILL NEED:

- a cloth napkin (ironed and perhaps starched)

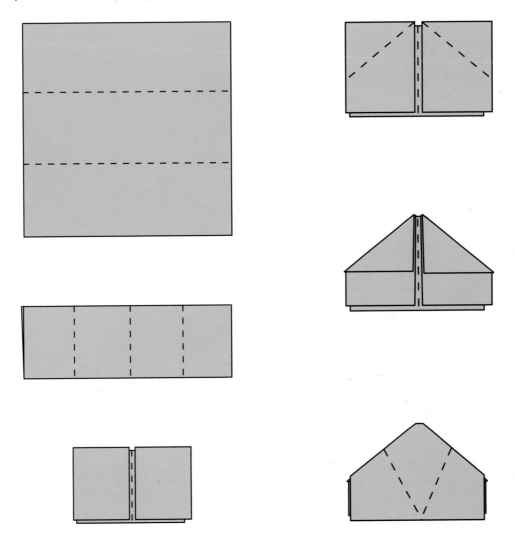

1. **Place** the napkin down flat, with the stitched turned-up side facing up. 2. **Fold** it in thirds, bringing the sides in toward the center. 3. **Fold** it in fourths, bringing the sides into the center. 4. **Fold** the upper corners toward the center to form a tent shape. 5. **Turn** the napkin over, with the point upward. 6. **Fold** it in thirds by folding each bottom corner diagonally across to its opposite edge. 7. **Insert** the second corner into the fold made by the first corner. 8. **Turn** the folded napkin over, stand it up, and shape it.

Metal Candleholders

YOU WILL NEED:

- multi-purpose epoxy putty or air-drying modeling clay
- pieces of open-work metal (such as one finds on various kitchen utensils and accessories)
- thumbtacks
- candles

1. Prepare some of the putty or clay according to the package directions. Place it in the center of one metal piece. Push a thumbtack into the center of the putty or clay (point upward). Leave to dry. **2. Insert** a candle onto the pin. **3. Repeat** steps 1 and 2 for each candleholder you wish to make.

My Pink Teddy

YOU WILL NEED:

- pink carded wool roving and/or top
- purple carded wool roving and/or top
- a felting needle
- a foam cushion (a piece of dense foam rubber, 1½ to 2 inches thick)

- purple felt
- scissors
- purple thread
- a needle

Make the teddy's body limb by limb. Then attach the various limbs together, using a felting needle.
1. The head: take a little pink wool. Shape it roughly with your fingers. Place it on the foam and poke it until you get a round ball. In the same fashion, make a second smaller round ball for the muzzle. Take a very small amount of purple wool, shape it with your fingers, place it on top of the muzzle and prick it to felt and fix it. Fix the muzzle to the head by pricking deeply. Take a very small amount of purple wool and shape it with your fingers to make the eyes. Place them on the head and prick them to felt and fix them. **2. The ears:** take a little pink wool (less than for the head) and shape it with your fingers. Place it on the foam and prick it until you get a round, flat shape. Make the second ear to match. Prick them with the needle to fix them to the head. **3. The body:** take some pink wool (slightly more than you used for the head) and shape it with your fingers. Place it on the foam and prick it until you get a large oval ball. **4. The limbs:** take some pink wool and shape it with your fingers to make a little sausage shape. Place it on the foam and prick it. Add a little pink wool to one of the ends to make a hand or a foot. Take a very small amount of purple wool, shape it with your fingers, and prick it on the bottom side of the hand or foot. Make the three other limbs in the same way. **5. Attach** the limbs to the body, by pricking them deeply into place, then attach the head in the same way. **6. Trace** out two (front and back) of the jacket pattern (see p. 308) on the purple felt, checking first to make sure it is the correct size for your completed felted bear. **7. Cut** out both ⅓ of an inch from the edge, and sew them together as front and back. Turn the jacket inside out so the seams are hidden. Carefully cut up the front middle of the jacket and turn back and sew the edges to finish so they won't fray. **8. Dress** the teddy.

Chessboard

YOU WILL NEED:

- a square piece of cardboard (18½ x 18½ inches)
- acrylic paint: turquoise, purple, white
- a small paintbrush
- pencil for tracing chess piece patterns
- 32 flat pebbles

To make the chessboard: 1. Trace out a grid of 2-inch squares (8 squares x 8 squares), taking care to leave a 1¼-inch border around all four edges of the cardboard. **2. Paint** every other square purple and leave to dry. Then paint the rest of the squares turquoise. Letting the first color dry before proceeding with the second will prevent smudging between squares of different colors. **3. When** everything is dry, use a thin paintbrush to tidy up the edges of any squares that require it. **4. Paint** the border white. Leave to dry.

To make the chessmen: 5. Trace two king patterns, two queen patterns, four rook patterns, four bishop patterns, four knight patterns, and sixteen pawn patterns (*see p. 307*) onto the pebbles. **6. Paint** one set purple and the other turquoise. Leave to dry. **7. Place** finished pieces on the chessboard.

Napkin Ring

YOU WILL NEED:

- 4 loopie cords (tubular, hollow plastic lace): 2 golden, 2 transparent with glitter
- 2 (4-hole) copper-colored bars
- a large multifaceted bead
- scissors

1. Make a rough knot with the ends of the four cords and start a round four-thread boondoggle (*see pp. 297 to 300*) 1½ inches long. **2. Undo** the knot. **3. Slip** the threads through one of the bars, with a golden cord going through the top hole, the two transparent cords through the middle two holes, and the second golden cord through the bottom hole. **4. String** the bead onto one of the transparent cords and then thread all four cords through the other bar, following the same order of colors. **5. Continue** the round boondoggle for another 1½ inches. **6. Knot** the golden cords to close the napkin ring. **7. Cut** off the excess transparent cords and the golden cords after the knots.

Just a Gulp Left

YOU WILL NEED:

- clear glass drinking glasses
- dishwashing liquid or white spirits
- Vitrea 160 colors: frosted pink, frosted orange, frosted red, frosted purple
- Vitrea 160 dilutant (optional)
- a soft, flat paintbrush

1. Use dishwashing liquid or white spirits to clean grease from the glasses. Use the paintbrush to paint the outside base of each glass in the color of your choice. (Vitrea 160 paints are a thermo-hardening, water-based paint designed for use on glass.) Leave to dry. Apply a second coat if the color is not deep enough. Allow the paint to dry for 24 hours. **2. Place** the glasses upside down in the oven. Fire them at 325°F for 40 minutes. Take the glasses out of the oven and let them cool at room temperature. This paint for glass is designed to be fired in a domestic oven. It is also dishwasher resistant.

Sugar Vases

YOU WILL NEED:

- several glass sugar shakers of different shapes and heights
- a drill with a metal bit
- fresh flowers

1. Use the drill to slightly widen some of the holes in the lids, taking care not to damage the neighboring holes. **2. Insert** a single stem into each of the enlarged holes.

Pretty Scents

YOU WILL NEED:

- 3 black pebbles
- acrylic paint: red, orange, brown
- a small paintbrush

- a packet of potpourri
- a colored varnished earthenware bowl

1. Paint drops on the pebbles; orange on one, red on the second, and brown on the third. Press down firmly with the paintbrush so that you leave traces of the brush, which will give a textured effect to make the drops look like seeds. **2. Place** the potpourri in the bowl and the painted stones on top of it.

Glittery Vase

YOU WILL NEED:

- thin paper printed with pink and orange patterns
- a vase
- adhesive varnish
- a flat paintbrush
- frosted relief paint

1. Tear the paper into pieces. Cover part of the vase with the adhesive varnish. Place the pieces of paper on the vase in an overlapping fashion. Apply a thin coat of adhesive varnish on top of the pieces of paper as you go. **2. Cover** the whole of the outside of the vase in this way, one area at a time. Leave the vase to dry. **3. Apply** a thin line of relief paint running along certain tears and certain motifs. Leave to dry. **4. Apply** a final coat of adhesive varnish over the entire surface.

Pimento Tequila Glasses

YOU WILL NEED:

- paper with pimento motifs
- scissors
- tequila glasses
- a flat paintbrush
- adhesive varnish
- spray acrylic or polyurethane (as a sealant)

1. Carefully cut out the pimento motifs. **2. Apply** a coat of adhesive varnish to a glass. Place the pimentos on the glass in a harmonious manner. Cover with adhesive varnish. Leave to dry. **3. Apply** a second coat of adhesive varnish for evenness. **4. Repeat** the process for the other glasses. **5. Following** the directions on the product, spray a coat of sealant so that you will be able to clean the glasses gently by hand. Leave to dry.

Wound-up Candle Jars

YOU WILL NEED:

- 2 colored-glass candle jars: 1 pink, 1 blue
- glue
- 4 loopie cords (tubular plastic craft laces): two pink, two blue
- scissors
- a toothbrush

1. Cover the surface of the candle jar with glue, leaving ¼ of an inch (or a little less) free at the top.
2. Carefully wrap a pair of loopie cords around the jar and hold them down firmly while the glue dries.
3. Cut off any excess cord. **4. The** next day, when the glue is really dry, rub off any excess glue traces with a toothbrush.

Lavender Heart Tray

YOU WILL NEED:

- a heart-shaped tray made of white wood
- primer paint (such as gesso)
- fine-grain sandpaper
- lavender-colored acrylic paint
- flat-backed glass pebbles
- plaster of paris
- strong wooden craft stick
- matte spray acrylic varnish
- a sheet of glass or acrylic cut to fit the inside of the tray (optional)

1. **Cover** the tray with a layer of primer (such as gesso). Leave it to dry. 2. **Lightly** sand the tray with fine-grain sandpaper. Wipe off. 3. **Paint** the tray lavender. Leave it to dry. 4. **Paint** the curved side of the pebbles with the lavender-colored paint. Leave to dry. 5. **Take** care, for the next stage must be carried out quickly yet precisely, because the plaster will set rapidly. Prepare a small amount of plaster of paris in a plastic container according to the manufacturer's instructions. Stir the plaster with a wooden stick. Immediately pour it into the tray and arrange the pebbles in it in a harmonious manner. Push them gently into the plaster and check that they are all at the same height for a uniform flatness. Leave to dry. 6. **Apply** a coat of matt spray varnish. Leave it to dry. 7. **If** the finished tray is not flat enough for your uses, use a piece of glass or acrylic cut to fit the inside of the tray. Ensure that the edges of this piece are rounded off to prevent cuts.

Butterfly Candle Jars

YOU WILL NEED:

- paper with flower and butterfly motifs
- scissors
- 3 glass candle jars with candles
- adhesive varnish
- a flat paintbrush

1. Carefully cut out the flowers and the butterflies. **2. Apply** one coat of adhesive varnish to a candle jar, one area at a time. Place the cutouts on top of the appropriate area and apply a coat of adhesive varnish on top of it. Leave it to dry. **3. Apply** a coat of adhesive varnish over the whole outside of the candle jar for evenness, then leave it to dry. **4. Repeat** entire process for the other candle jars.

Wooden Spool Candlesticks

YOU WILL NEED:

- wooden spools (slightly varying sizes okay)
- strong glue
- thin plywood
- a pencil
- a jigsaw
- fine-grain sandpaper
- small nails (optional)
- a hammer (optional)
- cardboard box
- spray paint: orange, pink, red
- 3 pillar candleholders

1. Place the spools on top of each other, preferably with the widest at the bottom. Once they are arranged as you wish, stick them together with the strong glue. Draw rounded X-shaped bases on the thin plywood and cut to shape with the jigsaw. Sand down any splinters or rough edges with the fine-grain sand paper. Glue the bases to the columns of reels, or use nails to attach them from the bottom up. **2. Place** one of the candlesticks in a cardboard box and spray it completely with one of the paint colors. Do the same for the other ones, changing the color for each candlestick. Leave them to dry. **3. Sand** the pillar candleholders (which will probably be gilded) so that they lose their shine and to give them a patina. Use the strong glue to stick the candleholders atop the candlesticks.

Zipper Vase

YOU WILL NEED:

- 13 zippers in multiple colors to make a 9-inch circumference vase
- matching thread
- a straight vase
- pins
- sewing machine
- scissors

1. **Select** zippers that are as long as the vase (in this case 8 inches tall). Pin two zippers together and straight-stitch them together, using the sewing machine. Add a third zipper, pin, and sew it. Assemble the rest of the zippers in the same way, until you have enough to cover the vase. 2. **To assemble** the first and last zippers, pin them together as before. Sew them together closed. When the sewing machine's presser foot is caught by the zipper's pull tab, lift up the foot, open the two zippers, and complete the stitching. 3. **Slip** any remaining threads inside, knot them and cut off the excess. You can adapt this vase holder to a shorter vase by opening the zippers.

My Zen Garden

YOU WILL NEED:

- 3 round pebbles
- acrylic paint: pink, sky-blue, mauve, white
- a paintbrush
- a fan brush

- a rectangular glass dish
- clean, dry sand
- a mini-rake or fork

1. Paint the entire surface of each pebble: one pink, one sky-blue, and one mauve. Leave them to dry.
2. Use a fan brush to paint a white swirl on each pebble. Leave to dry. **3. Place** the sand in the glass dish.
Use a mini-rake or a fork to trace curves in the sand. Place the pebbles where you like on the sand.

Watering Can Vase

YOU WILL NEED:

- paper napkins with tulip motifs
- scissors
- a galvanized steel watering can
- adhesive varnish
- a flat paintbrush

1. Carefully cut out the tulip motifs, keeping only the top layer. **2. Cover** part of the watering can with adhesive varnish. Place the tulips on the watering can (with the bottom of their stems in line with the base rim). Cover them with adhesive varnish. **3. Place** one tulip after another until you have gone completely around the watering can. Make sure that you cover the entire surface of the watering can with the first coat of adhesive varnish to avoid any differences in shine. Leave to dry. **4. Apply** a second coat of adhesive varnish to the entire surface for evenness.

Plate for Chocolates

YOU WILL NEED:

- paper with chocolate motifs
- scissors
- a glass plate
- adhesive varnish

- a flat paintbrush
- a can of gold spray paint
- spray acrylic or polyurethane (as a sealant)

1. Carefully cut out the chocolate motifs. **2. Turn** the plate upside down and work on the underside. Apply a coat of adhesive varnish to the whole of the underside of the plate and place the motifs on the rim in a harmonious fashion. Apply a coat of adhesive varnish over the cutouts and the entire surface of the plate rim. Leave it to dry. **3. Spray** the entire underside of the plate with gold paint. Leave it to dry. **4. Following** the directions on the product, spray a coat of sealant so that you will be able to clean the plate gently by hand. Leave it to dry. **5. Turn** the plate over and place real chocolates on it.

Decorated Paperweights

YOU WILL NEED:

- 3 flat pebbles of different sizes
- a pencil
- acrylic paint: spring-green, emerald-green, turquoise-blue
- a small paintbrush
- relief acrylic paint: metallic-orange, silver
- a glue gun and glue sticks
- 3 tiny fabric cushions (mini pillows filled with weighted matter)

1. With a pencil, mark off three horizontal strips on each pebble. Paint each of the parts in either spring-green, emerald-green, or turquoise-blue, using the photo above as inspiration. Leave them to dry. **2. Trace** out the flowers (*see p. 304*) on the pebbles with a pencil. Paint them different colors with the acrylic paint and leave to dry. **3. Then** use the relief paint to mark the line between the different colors, taking care to avoid the flower. Leave them to dry. **4. Glue** each pebble to the center of a cushion. Use the cushions on top of stacks of paper napkins, paper plates, or paperwork.

Colorful Coaster

YOU WILL NEED:

- 30 dry yellow lentils (per coaster)
- acrylic paint in a variety of colors
- a small paintbrush
- crystal resin
- resin hardener
- a small plastic pot (such as a film canister)
- a larger plastic pot
- a small plastic spoon
- round silicone mold (4 inches in diameter) (one per coaster)
- colored sequins
- wooden craft stick
- a flat stick (such as a popsicle stick)

1. Paint the lentils in a variety of colors using the acrylic paint and leave them to dry. **2. Use** the small plastic pot as a measurer and pour two parts crystal resin and one part hardener into the larger plastic pot. Stir slowly with the spoon to prevent the formation of bubbles. Half-fill the silicone mold with the resin and leave to dry for approximately 12 hours. **3. Place** the lentils and sequins in circular or other imaginative patterns on the partially hardened resin disk. Cover them with resin mixed with hardener to the same proportions as before, use the stick to make sure everything is evenly covered with the resin, and leave to dry for 24 hours. Turn out each resin disk once it has hardened fully.

Cutting Board Shelves

YOU WILL NEED:

- wooden cutting boards
- shelf brackets (2 per cutting board)
- a drill
- screws

1. Position the shelf brackets on the bottom side of the cutting boards, checking that they are equally spaced on each of the boards. Screw the brackets onto the boards. **2. Screw** the bracketed shelves onto the wall.

Paris Memories

YOU WILL NEED:

For the model presented below (9½ x 7½ inches) you will need:

- a wooden shadow box frame
- silver spray paint
- imitation leather fabric
- a ruler
- a ballpoint pen
- scissors
- double-sided sticky tape
- pink glitter glue gel
- a glue gun or strong glue gel
- decorative flower rhinestones
- silver or blue metal wire
- round-nose pliers
- two blue beads
- blue feathers
- Paris postcards
- decorative heart
- a round metal disk (e.g. a cover for a small container)
- flat-backed blue marbles
- a small blue Eiffel tower

1. Spray the box frame with two coats of silver paint. Leave it to dry. **2. Measure** the inside bottom of the box. Trace out the dimensions of the box on the reverse of the piece of imitation leather fabric and cut it out. Use the double-sided sticky tape to fix the piece to the bottom of the box. **3. Apply** pink glitter gel around the bottom and inside top edges of the frame. Glue the little flower gems onto the top and side edges of the frame (see photo). **4. Cut** two lengths of metal wire (approximately 8 to 10 inches long each) and twist one end of each into a spiral (using the pliers). Take two beads, glue a feather to each, then attach these to the other ends of the metal wires. Glue the completed decorations onto the bottom edge of the frame (with a spot of glue on the back of the beads). **5. Cut** images from the postcards and glue them onto the imitation leather inside the bottom of the box, along with the heart, the metal disk, and the flat marbles (glue the postcard of the dancer onto the metal disk). Place the little Eiffel tower on the bottom edge of the frame.

Fish Fancy

YOU WILL NEED:

- thick nickel-silver wire (approximately 50 inches)
- thin nickel-silver wire (numerous short lengths)
- wire cutters
- a glue gun and glue sticks
- twigs and pieces of driftwood
- string of fairy lights with 20 round pink bulbs
- limpet shells
- a tin of preserved fish (must show picture of fish on tin)
- tin snips
- a small nail
- a hammer

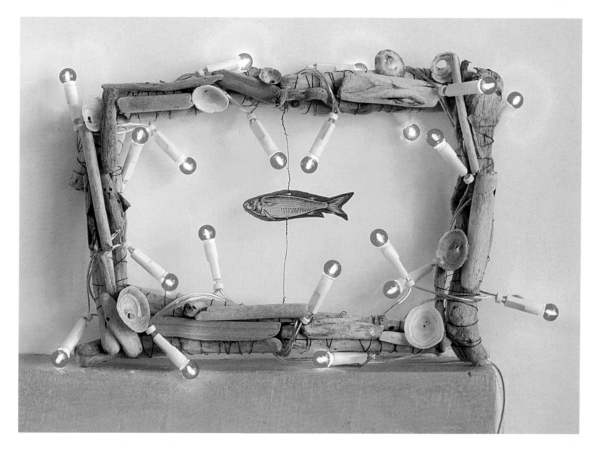

1. Use the thick nickel-silver wire to make a rectangle measuring 12 x 8 inches. Make several turns of the wire until the base is rigid, then fix the strands together using small pieces of thin metal wire. **2. Glue** some of the twigs and pieces of driftwood around the edge of the frame, spreading them out evenly. **3. Wrap** the string of fairy lights around the frame, centering the wire in the middle of each side, and attach it firmly using small pieces of thin metal wire. Glue more pieces of driftwood on top, followed by a few limpet shells. **4. Open** the tin of preserved fish, empty it, and wash it under hot water. After having dried the tin, use the tin snips to cut out the image of the fish printed on it. Make two little holes in the fish, centered on top and bottom (see photo), using a small nail and a hammer. Attach two lengths of thin metal wire to the fish and fix it to the top and bottom of the frame.

Plastic Parts Mobile

YOU WILL NEED:

- a utility knife and cutting mat
- pieces of perforated plastic (such as tops from containers of fancy sea salt, grated Parmesan cheese, scouring powder, drain filters, and commercial-sized containers of herbs, etc.)
- spray paint in several colors
- a mini-drill
- thin metal rods
- round-nose pliers
- large jump rings

1. Use the utility knife to cut the plastic stem from any plastic pull tabs. In order to vary the shapes when using identical pieces, keep only the round central part and remove some or all of the fins. With the other pieces of plastic, such as pourers, remove the flaps that hide the cutouts and holes. **2. If** you like, you can also spray paint some of the plastic pieces in order to get a nice mix of colors. **3. Pierce** a hole with the mini-drill through the edge of each piece. **4. Wrap** each end of a thin metal rod around the round-nose pliers to make loops. Use the jump rings to hang a plastic piece from each end of the rod. Place the rod on the end of your finger to find the balance point. Place the rod on the round-nose pliers at this point and bend each end of the rod downward. Adjust each end of the rod, by bending it up or down, until it is well balanced — when the rod is properly balanced it should swivel around the balance point on the end of your finger, making a circle in the air. If the balance is not quite right, then simply raise or lower one of the ends of the rod a little to correct the imbalance. Make several such groupings. **5. Attach** them one after another, using jump rings to connect one vertical rod to the one above it. Place a single plastic piece at the bottom of the last vertical rod.

Old-time Ads

YOU WILL NEED:

- old magazines containing advertisements
- differently shaped metal covers
- a pencil and eraser
- scissors
- double-sided sticky tape
- a sheet of decorative stickers
- a glue gun or glitter glue gel
- colored pencils or crayons
- little magnets
- decorations to be stuck onto the magnets and the covers: retro buttons, rhinetones, beads, fabric flowers, braiding, suspender buckles, small advertisements, candy
- poster putty or small self-adhesive hooks

1. Search garage sales and second-hand goods markets for old magazines containing images to cut out or photocopy (in color) and stick to the various metal covers. **2. Take** a metal cover, place it on an image, trace around it with a pencil and cut it out. Fix strips of double-sided sticky tape onto the metal cover and attach the image to it. **3. Decorate** with self-adhesive stickers, the glitter glue gel, or any other items. Color any black and white images using the colored crayons. **4. Make** fancy magnets by sticking different decorations onto them and placing the magnets on top of the images on the metal covers. Place the poster putty or self-adhesive hooks on the back of the metal covers, then make your own composition on the wall.

Blackboard Box

YOU WILL NEED:

- an old drawer measuring 11 inches x 8 inches
- dark-pink acrylic paint
- a flat paintbrush
- old prints or magazines
- glossy acrylic medium
- blackboard paint
- a ballpoint pen
- a ruler
- 5 gilded hook screws (⅛ inch diameter)
- school chalk (to write on the blackboard)

1. **Paint** the drawer pink and leave it to dry. Repeat for a second coat. 2. **Tear** out small pieces from magazines or prints (or photocopy them if you wish to preserve the originals). Stick them onto the edges of the drawer by painting the acrylic medium over them. Leave to dry. 3. **Paint** the inside bottom of the drawer with blackboard paint and leave it to dry. Repeat for a second coat. 4. **Mark** the center of the bottom edge of the drawer with a ballpoint pen. Make two other marks on each side of the central mark, spaced 2 inches apart (for a total of five equally spaced dots). Screw the gilded hooks into these marked spots. Use chalk to write your own message on the blackboard.

Fish Mobile

YOU WILL NEED:

- plastic tatting shuttles (fish shape or other interesting shape)
- mini-drill and drill bit
- jump rings
- metal rods
- round-nose pliers
- wire cutters

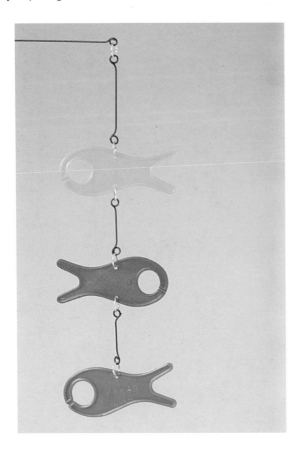 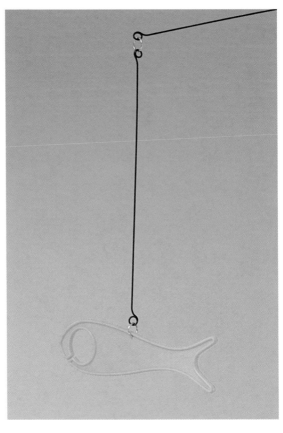

1. Drill a hole on the edge of each of the shuttles, taking care to ensure that the shape will hang horizontally by drilling it in the middle of the back. Place one jump ring in the hole. **2. Wrap** each end of a metal rod around the round-nose pliers to make loops. Use the round-nose pliers to make a small loop in the center of each wire you plan to use for horizontal mobile pieces. Use the jump rings to hang a shuttle from each end of the horizontal rod. Place the rod on the end of your finger to find the balance point. Place the rod on the round-nose pliers at this point and bend each end of the rod downward. Adjust each end of the rod by bending it up or down until it is well balanced. When the rod is properly balanced, it should swivel around the balance point on the end of your finger, making a circle in the air. If the balance is not quite right, then simply raise or lower one of the ends of the rod a little to correct the imbalance. Make several such groupings. Use the wire cutters to vary the length of the vertical wires. **3. Attach** the groupings one after another, placing a vertical rod between each one. Use a jump ring to attach each rod to the shuttle or to the rod below it. Place a single shuttle at the bottom of the last vertical rod.

River Rock Mirror

YOU WILL NEED:

- an untreated pine frame containing a mirror
- yellow acrylic paint
- a paintbrush
- a utility knife blade

- unpolished, flat river rocks
- a glue gun and glue sticks
- mother-of-pearl buttons

1. Cover the whole surface of the frame (including the edges) with two coats of acrylic paint, taking care not to get any paint on the mirror. If you get any paint on the mirror, scrape it off afterward using the utility knife blade. **2. Once** the paint has dried completely, use the glue gun to attach the pebbles to the frame. Cover the entire frame, taking care to leave as few gaps as possible between the pebbles. **3. Use** the glue gun to stick the mother-of-pearl buttons on top of the pebbles.

Plastic Spoon Chandelier

YOU WILL NEED:

- 225 plastic gelato spoons (with flat tips, see photo)
- a mini-drill and drill bit

- 225 jump rings
- a 10-inch diameter silver-plated metal ring (such as those used to make lampshades)

1. Drill holes through both ends of two-thirds of the spoons. Drill a single hole through the handle end of the remaining spoons. **2. Use** two jump rings to link three spoons of different colors together vertically. **3. Use** a single jump ring to hang each trio of spoons onto the lampshade ring.

Princess Window

YOU WILL NEED:

- air-drying modeling clay (e.g. Lyra Keramiplast Modeling Material)
- metal wire
- wire cutters
- fine sandpaper
- acrylic paint: white, red, pink
- small flat paintbrushes (various sizes)
- tiny paintbrush (for detail painting)
- thin black permanent marker (such as a fine-point Sharpie)

- glossy acrylic medium
- pieces of fabric: (different fabric and textures)
- small pieces of fancy ribbon
- scissors
- 2 small buttons
- pink glitter glue gel (in a tube)
- gold spray paint
- two round beads (crown and necklace)
- a storage box for CDs (without front or back wall) (8 x 8 inches)

The princess: 1. With the clay, mold the various parts of the princess separately following the directions on page 306. Once completed and dry, sand it down with the fine sandpaper. **2. Mix** the pink and white to paint the face and the hands. Paint the hair pink and the body red. Use a fine paintbrush to paint the details on the face. Once the paint is dry, use the black felt-tip to draw in the eyes. Give the figure a coat of glossy medium (using a medium-sized brush). **3. Cut** out small pieces of fabric and use the medium to stick them to the body at interesting angles. Leave to dry. Cut out bits of ribbon to stick around the wrists and to make the neckline. Fix them in place with a acrylic medium and add a button. Spread some glitter gel with your finger, tracing little spirals to decorate the dress. **4. Spray** the crown with gold paint and glue a bead into its center. Glue the crown to her head. Make a little necklace using a bead and metal wire.

The box: 5. Sand the box down and paint it. Alternate coats of pink and white without putting too much paint on the brush, in order to get a light pink textured effect (let each coat dry before applying the next one). Use the glitter gel to trace out spirals on the three visible surfaces. Leave to dry.

Spindly Clock

YOU WILL NEED:

- wood fiberboard (at least a square foot and ½ inch thick)
- drawing compass
- pencil
- ruler
- a jigsaw
- fine sandpaper
- a drill and wood bits
- 12 knitting needles (of various colors and sizes)
- a clock mechanism
- acrylic paint: gray, blue
- medium and fine paintbrushes
- cyanoacrylate glue (e.g. Super Glue or Krazy Glue)
- clock hands (traditional with a tear-shape at the end)

1. Use the drawing compass to trace out a circle with a 5-inch radius (10-inch diameter) on the wood. Divide the circle into 12 equal parts, and draw faint pencil lines from the center of the circle to the marked edge. Cut out the circle using the jigsaw. Sand the edges. Drill a hole into the edge of the wood in the center of each of the 12 marked locations; the diameter of each hole must match that of the knitting needle to be placed in it. Drill a larger hole for the needle that will indicate 12 o'clock. Drill a hole in the center of the face to receive the clock mechanism. Paint the wood gray. Leave it to dry. **2. Apply** a little glue to the end of each knitting needle and place a little in each corresponding hole. Place each needle into its hole. **3. Shorten** the clock hands and trim the ends to make them rounded instead of tear-shaped. Paint them blue and leave them to dry. Fit the clock mechanism in place.

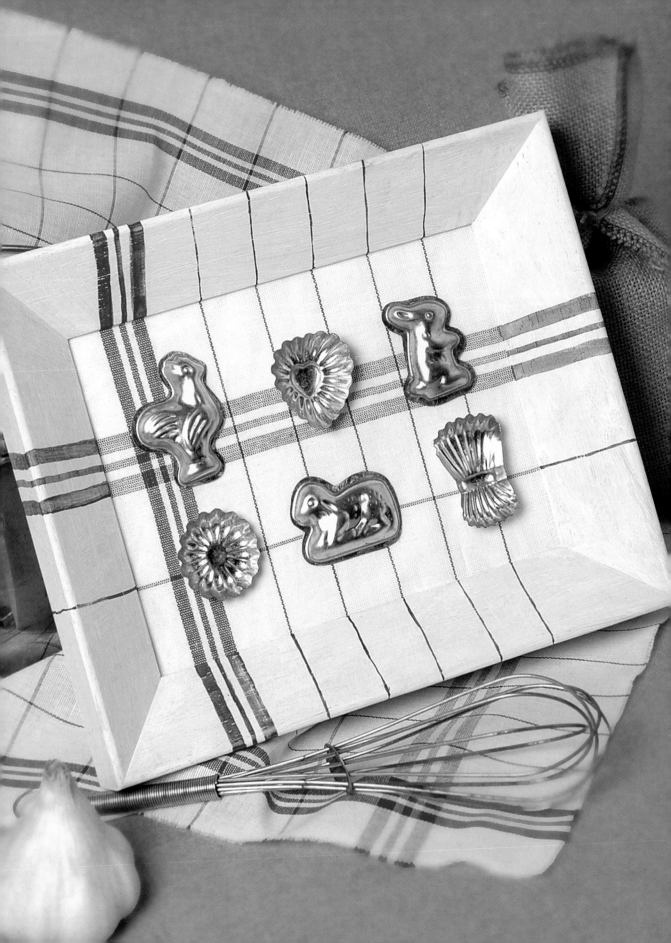

Chocolate Maker's Display

YOU WILL NEED:

For the model shown (9 x 10½ inches) you will need:

- a frame with wide edges
- acrylic paint: matte white, matte red
- paintbrushes of various sizes
- spray adhesive
- red and white dishcloth
- scissors
- a glue gun and glue sticks
- little chocolate molds

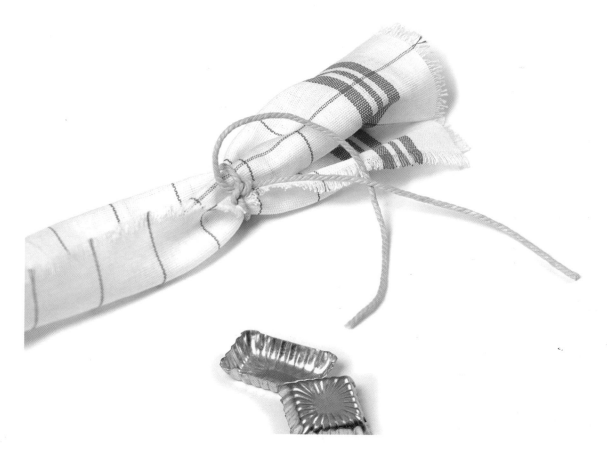

1. Dismantle the frame to remove the base. **2. Paint** the whole frame white using a large paintbrush, roughly covering it with a single coat to make it look less new. Leave it to dry. **3. Cover** the base of the frame (that you removed) with the spray adhesive and place it on the dishcloth, ensuring that it is in line with the grain. Choose one of the corners of the dishcloth so that you have thin and thick stripes. Trim the dishcloth around the edge of the frame, leaving an excess of ¼ of an inch. **4. Fold** the excess over the back and reattach the base to the frame. **5. Use** the thin paintbrush to paint thin red lines onto the edges of the frame. Use the small brush to do the same for the thicker stripes. **6. Use** the glue gun to put a drop of glue on each of the chocolate molds and place them within the frame.

Happy Birthday !

Boxes or Frames?

YOU WILL NEED:

- 6 blue shadow boxes (inside dimensions of 3½ inches square)
- large-grain sandpaper
- sheets of colored paper: white, pink, sky-blue, lime-green
- a pencil with eraser
- a ruler
- a utility knife and cutting mat
- burlap (3½ inches square)
- scissors
- spray adhesive
- 2 small flat pebbles, 1 large flat pebble
- acrylic paint: lime-green, pink, blue
- small paintbrushes
- a magazine
- shells
- flat marbles
- glass crystals
- resin shells and flowers
- a glue gun or thick glue in a tube

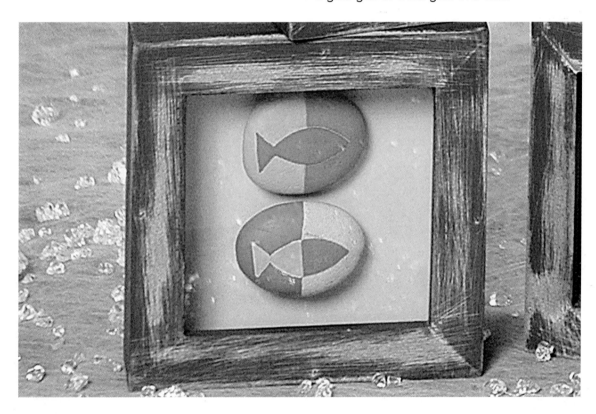

1. **Sand** the frames to distress the paint. 2. **Trace** out the following 3½-inch squares on the colored paper and cut them out: 1 white, 2 pink, 1 sky-blue, 1 lime-green. Also cut out a square from the burlap to the same dimensions. Cover the back of each square with spray adhesive and adhere one to each of the bases of the box frames as the background. 3. **Paint** all three pebbles with fish motifs in pink, green, and blue (see photos). Cut out a butterfly shape from a magazine of your choice (the butterfly shape in the illustration is cut from a magazine photo of a piece of embroidered cloth). 4. **Glue** all of your elements into the boxes of your choice. Be sure to glue the butterfly down only in its center so the wings can lift and create a shadow. 5. **Decorate** the last box with glass crystals. Add one stone and two resin shells. This last composition does not require any adhesive.

Grater Clocks

YOU WILL NEED:

- circular metal graters with different perforations
- clock mechanisms
- a drill with a ⅛-inch metal bit
- thick gloves
- flat clock hands
- red spray paint
- thumbtacks with red heads
- a glue gun and glue sticks

For the variant, you will also need:

- trivets with holes
- a metal washer
- a magnetic number

1. Drill the center of the graters with a ⅛-inch bit to allow for the fitting of the clock mechanisms. Make sure that you use gloves to hold the graters while you drill. If the grater is slightly conical, then place the pointed side upward so that the hands will be able to rotate normally. **2. Fit** the clock mechanism onto the grater. Paint the clock hands red. Leave them to dry, then fit the hands to the mechanism. **3. You** may fit red drawing pins or red-headed pins (with most of the shaft removed) to mark the principal hours. Slide them through the holes and attach them on the reverse using the glue gun.

Variant: Since the central hole is quite large, place a metal washer on top of it so that you can install the clock mechanism. Paint the clock hands red and install them before placing the magnetic number.

Ivy and Roses

YOU WILL NEED:

For this model (6¼ x 4¼ inches) you will need:

- a cream-colored wooden frame (1½ inches thick)
- large-grain sandpaper
- dry floral foam or styrofoam
- a utility knife and cutting mat
- glue (optional)

- 24 paper roses
- wire cutters
- double-sided sticky tape (very strong hold necessary)
- scissors
- brown raffia fronds
- 16 fabric ivy leaves

1. Use the sandpaper to sand off some of the paint finish and give the frame a worn look. **2. Cut** the foam to ⅓ of an inch thick and trim it so that it fits the inside shape of the frame. If the foam is packed down firmly, or wedged in place, you won't need to glue it. If necessary, glue the foam to the frame backing. **3. Use** the pliers to cut the rose stalks down to ½ of an inch long. Stick the roses into the foam and pack them tightly together in order to cover the foam completely. **4. Cut** strips of double-sided sticky tape ⅓ of an inch wide and stick them onto the inside edge of the frame opening. Fix the raffia fronds to the tape, cutting them off at the corners. **5. Stick** the ivy leaves around the edge of the frame, using small pieces of double-sided sticky tape.

New Baby Box Frame

YOU WILL NEED:

For the model shown (8 inches square) you will need:

- a pale-green box frame
- acrylic paint: white, yellow, mauve, pink
- a flat paintbrush
- air-drying modeling clay (e.g. Lyra Keramiplast Modeling Material)
- mauve pipe cleaners
- wire cutters
- mauve and pale-green taffeta
- spray adhesive
- a pencil with eraser
- pinking shears
- fine-grain sandpaper
- a small paintbrush
- pink glitter glue
- strong glue in a tube or a glue gun

1. Paint the inside of the box white. Apply a rough coat of white paint to the frame itself with a few strokes, just to give it a little texture. **2. Take** the air-drying clay and shape a heart measuring about 4 inches across. Smooth out the surface with a little water. Make two spirals on the ends of the mauve pipe cleaner. Snip the pipe cleaner in two with the wire cutters and stick them into the heart's point (see photo). Leave to dry. **3. Use** the spray adhesive to stick the mauve taffeta to the inside bottom of the box frame (fold the edges over the back). Place the now-dry heart on the green taffeta and trace out the shape of the heart ½ an inch larger than the outside edge. Cut out the heart with the pinking shears. Use the spray to stick it on top of the mauve fabric. **4. Remove** the spirals and sand down the heart. Apply two coats of yellow paint. Leave to dry. **5. Paint** the teddy's head mauve, then write your child's name underneath it. Finish the decoration. Trace around the contours of the head and muzzle with the glitter glue. Paint little polka dots on the mauve fabric with the glitter glue. Leave to dry. **6. Use** the strong glue to stick the heart in place. Stick the pipe cleaners in place with a spot of glue.

Forest Chandelier

YOU WILL NEED:

- branches of various thicknesses
- thick nickel-silver wire
- wire cutters
- a slice of wood (4-inch diameter, ½-inch thick)
- a mini-drill and drill bits
- a thin, wrought-iron candle chandelier ring (pictured) or a 10-inch silver-plated metal ring (such as those used to make lampshades)

- thick metal wire
- thin metal wire
- beads, glass test tubes, small plastic farm animals, fake decorative birds and butterflies, pinecones, dried flowers, small wood slices, twigs, whole nuts, acorns, dried flowers, etc.

1. To make the chandelier's central hanging point, cut six (6-inch) lengths from the largest branches and three (⅓-inch) lengths from a ⅛-inch-thick branch. Make sure that the longer pieces are all the same length, so that the chandelier hangs securely. Use the mini-drill to make holes ⅛ of an inch from each end of these long lengths of branch. Link these pieces together (top to bottom) in pairs by wrapping the thick nickel-silver wire through the holes multiple times. Make a central hole in the 4-inch slice of wood and three equidistant holes placed ⅓ of an inch from the edge. **2. Hang** each pair of branches from one of the holes. To do this, pass a piece (at least 12 inches long) of thick nickel-silver wire through the hole in one branch, fold the wire in half and twist it along its entire length. Pass the twisted wire through one of the holes in the 4-inch slice of wood, then through one of the short lengths of wood (⅓ of an inch long x ⅛ of an inch thick). Untwist the two strands of twisted wire and fold each one around the short length of branch, twisting them together again on the other side to secure the chandelier's hanging point. **3. To make** the central ceiling hold, take a length of thick metal wire and create a loop by folding a portion of the wire back on itself. Twist the wire around itself for a section after the loop. Pull the wire through the central hole in the 4-inch wood slice, leaving the loop underneath to hold the wire in place. **4. Cut** three (8-inch) lengths of thick nickel-silver wire. Pull a wire through each bottom hole previously drilled into the end of the bottom 6-inch branches. Attach the three wires by looping around evenly spaced points on the chandelier ring or lamp shade ring and twist securely to close in place. **5. Once** the ring is securely in place, use thin metal wire to attach all kinds of objects to the chandelier. Add to the chandelier seasonally or as you collect more items. Begin by adding sticks and dried flowers to cover or decorate the base of the chandelier. Use the mini-drill to make holes in the wood slices, the branches, the twigs, the nuts, the plastic animals, and other objects so that you can string them onto thin metal wire. Hang them on the chandelier by pulling the metal wire through the hole and twisting it around each piece. Hang the test tubes onto the chandelier by slipping a loop of metal wire around their necks and making a hook in the other end. The pinecones, and the decorative birds and butterflies may be hung using just a piece of twisted metal wire.

Frame of Friends

YOU WILL NEED:

For the model shown (8⅔ x 11 inches)
you will need:

- orange Japanese paper (19¾ x 25½ inches)
- purple Japanese paper (19¾ x 25½ inches)
- a shadow box frame
- a flat paintbrush
- glossy acrylic medium
- a ruler
- carpet tacks
- a hammer
- decorative metal wire (with beads)
- small pliers (for griping metal wire)
- a sheet of white paper (8½ x 11 inches)
- scissors
- a hole puncher
- purple raffia
- a black marking pen
- small clothespins
- passport photos of your friends

1. Tear the sheets of orange and purple Japanese paper down one side. Be sure to leave a small portion of orange paper for use in the heart created in step 4. Coat the inside bottom of the box and the frame with the acrylic medium, using the brush. Cover the whole of the bottom of the box with the two colors of paper, ensuring that the torn side runs down the center. Lay smaller pieces on top of them. Once the paper is dried, the medium will give it a transparent glaze effect. Leave it to dry. **2. Place** the carpet tacks on the inside edges, starting with the first one placed 1¼ inches from the top of the box. The remaining tacks should be placed at intervals of 2⅓ inches. They should not be nailed in all the way, since you must be able to wind the decorative wire around them. **3. Wind** the decorative wire around the tacks, as in the model shown in the photo. Then twist the wire back over itself to secure it, using the pliers. **4. Cut** out a heart shape (slightly larger than a passport photo) by laying a piece of the orange paper over the white paper. Use the acrylic medium to glue the two pieces together. Leave it to dry, then pierce a hole through which you can tie a small length of raffia. Write your message or caption on the heart using the black marking pen. **5. Use** the small clothespins to attach the photos of your friends to the lengths of decorative wire, along with the little heart, in a fashion similar to clothes on a line.

Mini Mirror

YOU WILL NEED:

- an aluminum lid (approximately 8–10 inches in diameter)
- a hammer
- strong glue
- a frameless round mirror (5 inches in diameter)
- black, blue, and green loopie cords (tubular plastic craft laces)
- cyanoacrylate glue (e.g. Super Glue or Krazy Glue)

1. Tap the bottom of the lid with the hammer to flatten it. **2. Spread** some of the strong glue behind the mirror. Center the mirror on the lid. Leave it to dry by placing heavy objects (such as heavy books) on top of it. **3. Wrap** the cords around the mirror to measure the exact length needed of each cord. Beginning with the black on the inside, wrap it, then a green cord, then another black, then blue on the outside edge. Use the cyanoacrylate glue to fix the colored cords in place around the mirror.

Fairy Wishes for Baby

YOU WILL NEED:

- a pencil
- 4 flat pebbles
- acrylic paint: pink, yellow, green, blue, brown
- an acrylic marking pen
- glue
- a wooden frame
- baby photo of your choice

1. Use a pencil to draw the fairy shapes (like those in the photo) on three of the pebbles. **2. Paint** the fairies, using the photo above for inspiration. **3. Write** the first name of your child on the fourth pebble in acrylic pen, as well as his or her date of birth or christening. Leave it to dry. **4. Glue** the three fairy pebbles on the sides and at the top of the frame. **5. Glue** the name pebble at the bottom of the frame. **6. Slip** a photo of your little one into the frame.

Wood, Beads, and Butterflies

YOU WILL NEED:

For the model shown (16 inches square)
you will need:

- pieces of dried wood
- pruning shears
- brown raffia (long lengths)
- a mounting fixture (to fix the frame to the wall)
- glue in a tube
- a variety of beads (to fix onto the ends of the branches)
- shells
- 6–8 butterflies mounted on stalks

1. Gather together pieces of dried wood to make the four sides of the frame. Choose the straightest ones and cut twelve (16-inch) lengths with pruning shears, then gather three pieces together for each side. Knot the four corners together with the raffia. Attach the mounting fixture to the back of the top piece of the frame. **2. Crisscross** the central part of the frame with the thinner twigs, wedging their ends between those forming the sides. **3. Cut** off any leafy bits and glue beads to the twig ends. Add the shells using touches of glue. **4. Attach** the butterflies by twisting the wire stalks around the twigs.

Forest Floor Frames

YOU WILL NEED:

- untreated pine frame (with a piece of frame glass) measuring 9½ inches square
- dark-oak wood stain
- a flat paintbrush
- a scroll saw
- branches of wood (1¼ inches in diameter)
- branches of wood (⅓ of an inch in diameter)
- a glue gun and glue sticks
- untreated pine frame (with a piece of frame glass) measuring 11½ x 9½ inches
- acorn caps
- small flat pliers (optional)

Wood slices frame: 1. Remove the glass from the square frame and set it aside. Apply an even coat of wood stain to the whole surface of the frame, including the outside edges, and leave it to dry. **2. Use** the scroll saw to cut ⅓-inch-thick slices from the two different sizes of branches. You can use a handsaw and miter if you do not have a scroll saw, but it takes longer. **3. Use** the glue gun to stick the larger slices of wood onto the frame, taking care to align them neatly. Place the smaller slices of wood between the larger ones and stick them in place using the glue gun. Replace the glass in the frame and insert the image of your choice.

Acorn frame: 1. Prepare the second wooden frame as you did the previous one. **2. Stick** the acorn caps onto the frame, using the glue gun to apply the glue to the rim of the caps. Do not use too much glue and take care not to burn your fingers with the glue when you apply it; you can use flat pliers to hold the acorn caps if you like. Cover the whole surface of the frame, taking care to alternate small and large caps. **3. Replace** the glass in the frame and insert the image of your choice.

It's a Snap

YOU WILL NEED:

- a flat-sided wooden frame
- silver paint
- a flat paintbrush
- sticky tape
- modeling clay
- an assortment of snaps
- epoxy resin
- a plastic pot
- a plastic spoon
- fine-grain sandpaper

1. Remove the sheet of glass from the center of the frame. Paint the frame silver, including the edges. Leave it to dry. **2. Place** strips of sticky tape around the edge of the window and the outer edge of the frame, slightly sticking up over the edge so as to form a kind of barrier. Fill in the corners with a little modeling clay to prevent any leakage. **3. Arrange** your snaps on the frame in a harmonious manner according to size, shape, and color. Then carefully remove them from the frame and place them to one side in the same order. **4. Mix** a little of the epoxy resin in a plastic pot. Epoxy resin comes in two containers, one containing the resin and the other a hardening agent, both of them liquids. The two parts are generally mixed according to a ratio of two parts hardener to one part resin. Pour the epoxy resin mixture onto the frame. Place the snaps back on the frame in the order you had arranged them. Leave to dry for 24 hours. **5. Remove** the modeling clay, as well as the sticky tape. Rub down any rough edges with the sandpaper.

Here Comes the Bride!

YOU WILL NEED:

For the model shown (12 x 16 inches)
you will need:

- a shadow box
- a pencil with eraser
- air-drying modeling clay (e.g. Lyra Keramiplast Modeling Clay)
- strong glue in a tube
- matte white acrylic paint
- a flat paintbrush (approximately 1¼ inches wide)
- photocopies of a musical score
- a little cherub
- 3 small fabric ivy leaves
- metal wire
- round-nose pliers
- a square bead
- a photo of the bride and groom
- 8 metal beads
- 4 large fancy beads
- 3 springs, each 1¾ inches long
- 2 small metal rings
- a white tassel
- a carpet tack
- a hammer

1. Trace interwoven initials on the bottom of the box in pencil. **2. Roll** a hazelnut-sized piece of paste between your fingers to soften it. Roll it on the table into a sausage shape. Place it on the pencil line, shape it into the letters then pinch it to fix it to the bottom of the box. Leave it to dry for a day. **3. Since** the letters will not have stuck securely to the box, you will need to fix them the next day with the strong glue. Paint the frame and inside bottom of the box white (use several coats), and immediately place small pieces of the photocopied musical score on the frame, which will stick to the paint. Leave to dry. **4. Glue** the little cherub to the inside edge of the frame, along with the three ivy leaves. **5. Use** the pliers to twist the metal wire into a spiral shape. Fix it into the square bead, then glue it next to the little cherub; the wire stalk will serve as a photo clip. **6. To make** the pendant, string a metal bead, a large fancy bead, a metal bead, and a spring onto a length of metal wire. Repeat this pattern three times total, making a bend in the wire after each set. Use the pliers to close off both ends. Take another piece of metal wire, bend it into an elegant spiral shape, and close off the ends. Attach the spiral to the pendant with a small metal ring. Use the second small metal ring to hang the white tassel from the last bead on the pendant. Attach the pendant to the frame with the carpet tack.

Alphabet Pebbles

YOU WILL NEED:

For the model shown (11 x 14 inches) you will need:

- a white shadow box with wide sides
- large-grained sandpaper
- 26 (or more) pebbles, relatively round and flat

- a pencil with eraser
- black acrylic paint
- a very fine paintbrush
- glossy spray varnish (optional)
- a glue gun and glue sticks

1. Sand the frame so that the paint flakes. Leave the sides in natural wood. **2. Place** four rows of five pebbles and one row of six pebbles in the inside bottom of the box. Vary the composition by choosing pebbles of different shapes and sizes. **3. Draw** one of the 26 letters of the alphabet on each of the pebbles with the pencil. Maintain your composition by moving the pebbles one by one and replacing them as you go. Paint the letters in black on the pencil line. Leave them to dry. **4. If you** wish to give your composition a more luminous look, apply a coat of varnish onto each painted pebble. Use the glue gun to glue each pebble in place.

Ladybug Chair

YOU WILL NEED:

- a wooden chair
- sandpaper
- primer paint (such as gesso)
- green acrylic paint
- a flat paintbrush
- paper napkins with ladybug designs
- scissors
- adhesive varnish

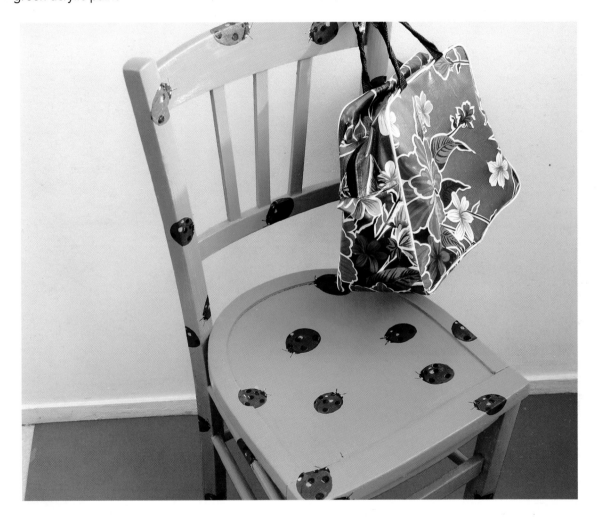

1. Lightly sand the chair with the sandpaper. Wipe off the dust. **2. Give** the whole chair one coat of primer. Leave it to dry. **3. Paint** the chair green. Leave it to dry. **4. Carefully cut** out the ladybug designs from the napkins and remove all but the top printed layer. **5. Cover** part of the chair with adhesive varnish. Place a ladybug on the varnished section of the chair and cover it with adhesive varnish. **6. Cover** the whole chair with ladybugs in this way; be sure to cover the whole chair with the first coat of adhesive varnish so as to avoid differences in shininess. Leave the chair to dry. **7. Give** the whole chair a final coat of adhesive varnish for evenness.

Stenciled Drawers

YOU WILL NEED:

- a wooden chest of drawers
- primer or acrylic paint (color to match the background color of stencil sheets)
- a flat paintbrush
- stencil sheets (enough to cover the entire surface area of your chest of drawers)
- a ruler
- scissors
- polyvinyl glue
- clear varnish

additional for variant:

- buttons
- hammer and nails

1. Paint the exterior surfaces of the chest of drawers the same color as the paper the stencils are printed on. Leave it to dry. **2. Measure** the surfaces to be covered with the stencil sheets. Cut out shapes from the stencil sheets to fit these various surfaces, but making each edge ⅓ of an inch smaller. **3. Glue** a small area of the surface to be covered. Carefully place one of the edges of the paper at the desired place. Use the ruler to press down the paper. Add more glue to the surface, lay down a little more of the sheet of paper, pressing down again with the ruler as you go. Continue in this fashion until you have covered the entire surface, taking care to leave as few creases and air bubbles as possible. Continue in this way until you have covered all of the sides of the chest of drawers. Leave it to dry. Varnish all surfaces (follow directions on the can of varnish).

Variant: Glue a large white button onto each of the wooden handles. For greater hold, fix small nails with heads through the buttonholes into the handles.

Fancy Stool

YOU WILL NEED:

- 2 round stools
- white acrylic paint
- a medium paintbrush
- little mother-of-pearl and pearly plastic buttons
- a red mother-of-pearl button
- cyanoacrylate glue (e.g. Super Glue or Krazy Glue)
- masking tape
- modeling clay
- epoxy resin
- plastic pot
- wooden craft stick
- a pin
- fine sandpaper

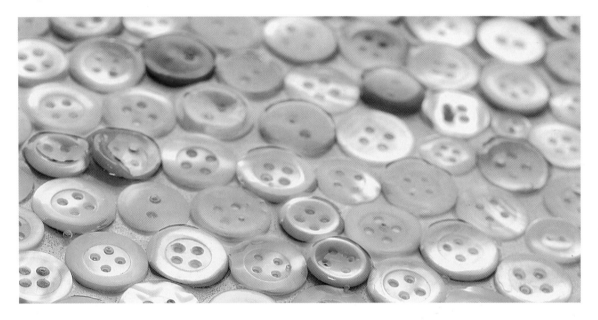

1. Paint the seat of each stool white. **2. Glue** the buttons on one by one, starting at the edge of the stools. Gradually cover the surface with concentric circles until you reach the middle of the seat. Mix up mother-of-pearl and pearly plastic buttons. Place the one red button somewhere off center on one of the stools. (**Tip:** It is a good idea to varnish the red mother-of-pearl button before pouring on the resin, since the dye tends to seep out.) **3. If** the stool does not have a rim, stick masking tape around it to form a kind of barrier to contain the resin. To make sure there is no leakage, add some modeling clay at the point where the tape meets the stool. **4. Mix** the epoxy resin in a plastic pot. The epoxy resin comes in two containers, one of which contains the resin, the other the fixative, both in liquid form. Mix together one part fixative to two parts resin. Try to avoid getting any air into the resin as your stir it, since this will create bubbles. Pour the resin onto the surface of the stool. Use a wooden craft stick to fill in the gaps between the buttons. If any bubbles appear (particularly in the holes of the buttons), pop them with a pin. Leave to dry for 24 hours. **5. Remove** the modeling clay and the masking tape. If the stool does not have a rim then sand down any raised edges using fine sandpaper.

A Good Seat

YOU WILL NEED:

- branches of wood in a range of diameters (between 1 inch and 1¾ inches)
- a scroll saw
- one medium wooden plank (approximately 13 inches square and ¾ inch thick)
- a drawing compass
- a glue gun and glue sticks
- a jigsaw
- thick, wide adhesive tape
- millefiori glass beads
- crystal resin
- resin hardener
- a plastic container
- a plastic spoon
- a pin (straight or safety)
- spring-green paint for metal
- a flat paintbrush
- metal stool legs
- fine sandpaper
- a small hand drill or wood gimlet
- wood screws

1. Use the scroll saw to cut numerous (⅕-inch-thick) slices from the branches of wood. **2. Trace** a 12½-inch diameter circle on the plank of wood using the drawing compass. Use the glue gun to stick the little slices of wood all over the surface of the circle until it is completely covered. The wood slices should cover the edge of the traced circle. Retrace the circle on top of the wood slices and cut out the disk using the jigsaw. **3. Wind** the thick adhesive tape around the wooden disk several times, pressing it down firmly so that it adheres well. The tape should protrude above the edge of the disk to form a stiff rim or mold. Place the little millefiori glass beads between the wood slices. Prepare the resin: mix the resin with the hardener in a plastic container according to the quantities suggested by the manufacturer. With the wood slice–covered wooden disk on a flat surface, carefully pour the resin into the mold, spreading it out evenly. Make sure that the wood slices are covered completely and leave to dry for 24 hours. Use the pin to prick any air bubbles that form. **4. Once** the resin has dried fully, remove the adhesive tape and apply two coats of the spring-green paint to the edge of the disk. **5. Sand** stool legs with fine sandpaper and apply two coats of the spring-green paint. Use the small hand drill to make screw holes in the disk, then fix the disk to the legs using the wood screws.

Unraveled

YOU WILL NEED:

- a wooden chair
- wood glue
- fine sandpaper (and a woodblock for a sander)
- black acrylic paint
- a small paintbrush
- thin cardboard (slightly larger than chair seat)
- a pencil
- 2 sheets of transparent, colorless acrylic (such as Plexiglass)
- double-sided sticky tape
- a jigsaw
- clamps
- a drill and wood bits
- spool of black thread
- 6 screws
- a screwdriver

1. Remove the seat from the wooden chair. Fill any holes with the wood glue. Leave the glue to dry, then sand it down. Paint the chair black and leave to dry. **2. Trace** out the shape of the seat on a sheet of thin cardboard to make a template. Fix the two sheets of acrylic and the template of the seat together with the double-sided tape. Cut out the sheets of acrylic to the shape of the stencil using the jigsaw. Then remove the stencil and the tape. Use the sandpaper wrapped around a piece of wood to carefully sand down the sheets of acrylic and smooth off any sharp edges and corners. **3. Use** the clamps to fix the sheets to the chair frame. Drill six holes through the acrylic and the chair frame — these will hold the screws that will keep the sheets of acrylic in place on the chair. Take off the sheets of acrylic and separate them. Remove the protective film from one of the sheets and lay the sheet on the chair frame. **4. Unravel** the black thread all over the bottom sheet of acrylic to create a swirly effect that becomes more concentrated in the center. Then remove the protective film from the second sheet of acrylic and lay the sheet on top of the first one without disturbing the black string. **5. Screw** the acrylic sheets into place on the chair to make a new seat. If the screws are not black, then paint them using a small paintbrush.

Handle It

YOU WILL NEED:

- a chest of drawers
- acrylic paint in different shades of blue
- a medium paintbrush
- teaspoons (one for each drawer)
- a drill with wood bits
- multipurpose epoxy putty

1. Most chests of drawers of this kind have a cutout piece that serves as a handle. If yours does not, turn the drawer around so you can screw a handle of your choosing into what was previously the back of the drawer. **2. Use** a range of blue shades to paint the chest of drawers. Cut or break off the handles of a number of teaspoons (one per drawer). **3. Since** the small ends of the spoon handles are more or less round, simply use a drill fitted with a wood bit of the corresponding diameter to the spoon handles to make holes in each of the drawers. Stick the broken end of the handle through the hole. Prepare the epoxy putty and shape a small piece to cover the part of the handle sticking out inside the drawer. Leave to dry.

Step Stool Redux

YOU WILL NEED:

- 4 plastic trays with varied designs and colors
- a jigsaw with a blade for cutting metal
- a wooden stool or small wooden table
- a ruler
- a pencil
- a file or rasp
- strong glue
- a spatula (for spreading glue)
- a clamp and weights
- medium-grain sandpaper
- paintbrushes
- acrylic paint: red, black

1. Roughly cut off the sides of the trays to leave only the flat part. Use the jigsaw fitted with the blade for cutting metal, which will cut this type of plastic much better than blades for cutting wood. **2. Measure** the stool's seat or the table's top. Work out the required size of the squares or plastic tile shapes. Measure and cut out four squares from the trays. File the edges to remove any plastic fibers that may be sticking out. **3. Use** the spatula to spread the glue on the seat of the stool or top of the table. Position the four tray tiles on top. Keep them in place using the clamp and the weights placed in the center until completely dry. Round off the corners with the file. **4. Use** the sandpaper to sand down the wooden parts of the stool. Remove all of the dust. Paint the stool red. Paint the top edge and the bottom 2 inches of the legs black.

Teaspoon Coat Hooks

YOU WILL NEED:

- 4 stainless steel teaspoons
- a hammer
- a drill with metal bits
- tape measure
- a vise
- screws
- a screwdriver

1. Make sure that you choose good quality stainless steel teaspoons (not too thin) fitted with flat handles to make drilling and attachment easier. If necessary, use the hammer to flatten the ridges in the handles a little. **2. Drill** two holes in each handle, spaced 2 inches apart. **3. Place** each spoon in the vise and use the hammer to bend them into right angles. **4. Screw** the spoons onto the post, wall, or board. Bend each spoon farther by hand until each one forms a rough V shape.

Blue Jeans Rug

YOU WILL NEED:

- 2 pair old blue jeans
- thread
- scissors
- pins
- sewing machine
- a famous label

1. Tear strips measuring approximately 32 to 34 inches long from the blue jeans. These strips should be between about 1½ and 3½ inches wide. Remove any excess threads on the ends and sides to make frayed edges. Place the strips next to each other, aiming for an interesting arrangement of colors. Turn some of the strips over so as to play with slightly different textures and hues. **2. Pin** one strip to another, then sew them together. Add another strip, pin and sew it, then do the same for the other strips. Sew all of the wider strips together first, then lay thinner strips on top — or else do the opposite. Cut off any excess thread but make sure the edges of the rug retain their "frayed jeans" look. Then sew around the edges of the rug to prevent it from fraying any further. **3. Add** the famous little red label removed from the seat of your favorite jeans.

Sweet Dream Blanket

YOU WILL NEED:

- a green blanket
- 3 self-adhesive letter Z patches for embroidering
- pins
- matching thread
- sewing machine

1. Center the letters in the middle of the blanket, but at least 12 inches from the top of the blanket so that they are not hidden by a turned-down sheet. **2. Remove** the adhesive protection from the letters and apply them. Pin the letters. Straight-stitch them with the sewing machine. **Tip:** use a single or twin bed blanket, since it will be easier to handle when stitching it with the sewing machine.

Hot Cherries!

YOU WILL NEED:

- about 18 oz. of cherry stones (washed and dried)
- ½ yard of flower-print cotton fabric
- ½ yard plain cotton fabric
- 36 inches cotton bias binding
- scissors
- sewing machine
- iron
- cotton thread to match the bias binding
- straight pins

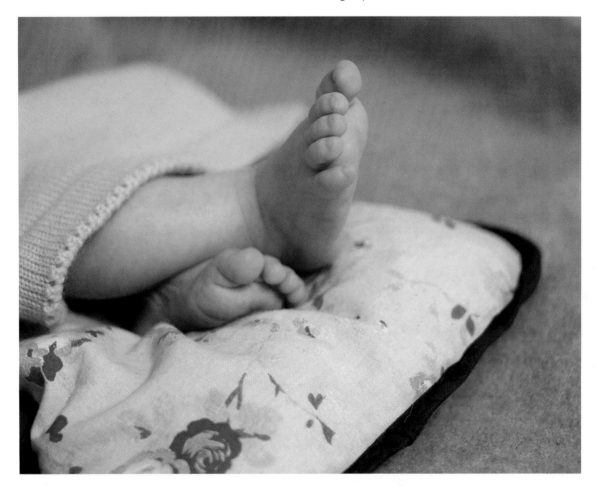

1. Cut two 8-inch squares (*see p. 309*), one from the flower-print fabric and one from the plain fabric, then round off all of the corners. Pin the two pieces of fabric right sides together and straight-stitch them together with the sewing machine. Leave a 1½-inch opening. Turn over and press, then fill the cushion with cherry stones. Hand stitch the opening closed with a basting stitch and then sew the bias around the edge of the pillow to cover the seam where the two pieces of fabric meet. **2. You** can use the pillow either hot or cold, by placing it in the fridge or in the microwave. When heated, the cushion will release a pleasant cherry scent. This is ideal for children, and they will be amused by the sound of the cherry stones gently rubbing together.

Desk on Wheels

YOU WILL NEED:

- 4 metal legs with wheels
- a tray with recesses
- a pencil
- a drill and drill bits
- red paint for metal

- a paintbrush
- turquoise-blue paint
- screws and nuts (to attach legs to underside of tray)

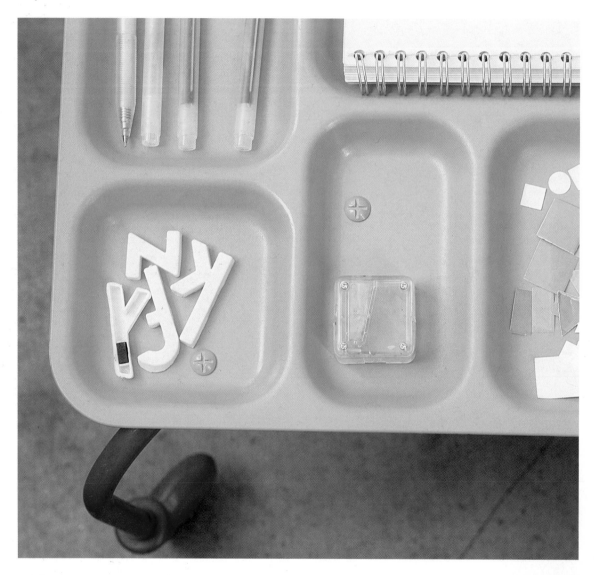

1. Place the tray on top of the legs, mark the spots where you will be fitting the screws and nuts, then drill holes in those spots. Apply two coats of red paint to the legs. **2. Paint** the tray turquoise blue, crisscrossing the coats to ensure an even finish. Leave to dry. **3. Fix** the legs to the tray with the screws and nuts. Paint the visible parts of the screws on the top of the tray.

Sky Lamp

YOU WILL NEED:

- 4 loopie cords (tubular, hollow plastic lace): 2 metal-gray, 2 sky-blue
- a slender lamp stand
- 8 large silver glass beads
- scissors

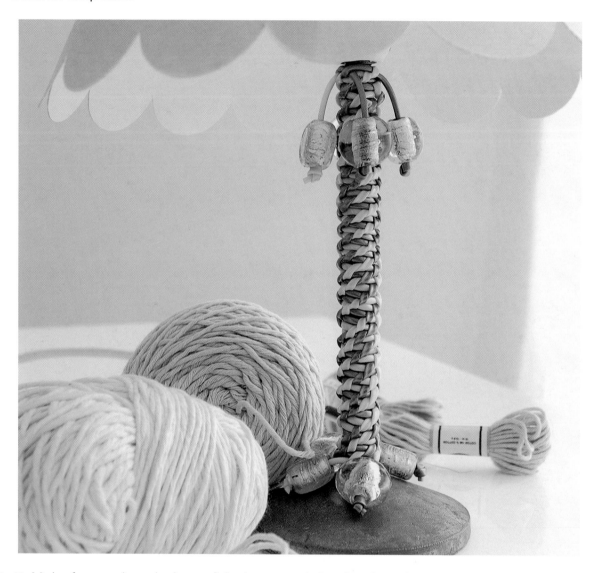

1. Hold the four cords at the base of the lamp stand, 2 inches from their ends. **2. Braid** a round four-cord boondoggle (*see p. 298*) from the base to the top of the lamp stand. **3. Slip** a bead onto each of the cords at the base, make a knot to hold each one close to the base, and cut off any excess. **4. Do** the same for the beads at the top, but make the knots at a distance of 2 inches from the lamp stand, then cut off any excess.

Letter Box

YOU WILL NEED:

- a cardboard shoe box
- cream-colored acrylic paint
- a flat paintbrush
- paper with printed motifs of envelopes, letters, pens, etc.

- scissors
- adhesive varnish
- a utility knife

1. Paint the inside and the outside of the shoe box cream (including the lid) and leave to dry. Apply a second coat of paint. **2. Carefully** cut out the various motifs. **3. Cover** part of the box with adhesive varnish. Place the first cutouts and cover them with adhesive varnish. Continue for the rest of the box and its lid. Leave to dry. **4. Glue** some of the cutouts over both the box and the lid. Leave to dry. Cut these cutouts with a utility knife to separate the box from its lid. **5. Apply** a final coat of adhesive varnish over the entire surface. Leave to dry.

Pincushion

YOU WILL NEED:

- a pencil or seamstress's chalk
- orange felt
- orange metallic thread
- orange thread
- cotton wool
- a ball of white felt
- orange seed beads
- scissors
- a needle

1. **Trace** out two disks measuring 4 inches in diameter on the orange felt. Cut ¼ inch from the edge. 2. **Use** the metallic thread to embroider four medians on one of the disks, using a front stitch (*see p. 305*). 3. **Place** the two disks on top of each other, right sides together, and sew them together around their edges, leaving a 2-inch opening. Turn inside out and fill with tightly packed cotton wool. Close with an invisible stitch. 4. **Wind** strings of seed beads (12 to 15 beads) around the ball of white felt, as in the photograph. Stitch the ball of felt crossways to keep the strings of beads in place. Make eight such strings of beads. 5. **Sew** the ball of felt into the middle of the pincushion.

All-in-One Sugar Canister

YOU WILL NEED:

- a metal canister with a lid
- a drill and sanding disk with plastic brushes
- spray varnish
- a metal drill
- a teaspoon (with most of its handle removed)
- air-drying modeling clay (e.g. Lyra Keramiplast Modeling Material)

1. Sand the exterior of the canister using the drill fitted with the sanding disk. **2. Varnish** the tin. **3. Use** the metal drill to make a hole in the center of the lid. Stick the end of the spoon's cut-off handle through this hole. Prepare the Shape a small piece of modeling clay and form to cover the part of the spoon handle sticking up through the lid. Leave it to dry.

X-Ray Containers

YOU WILL NEED:

- photocopier
- groups of office supplies for "x-raying": scissors of various sizes, paperclips, markers, and pens
- empty food cans of various sizes
- a utility knife and cutting mat
- thick card stock
- permanent spray adhesive
- double-sided sticky tape (1/3 inch wide)

1. Set the photocopier to the "negative" or the "negative/positive" black and white setting and photocopy the various elements by group. You may need to increase the contrast so as to obtain the minimum amount of gray. **2. Measure** the height and diameter of the cans, add 1/16 of an inch to the can's diameter measurements, and cut the "x-rays" to these final dimensions. Be sure to cut each "x-ray" to match the dimensions of the can in which you plan to store that office supply. **3. Cut** rectangles from the thick card stock to the same dimensions. Cover one side of each of the cut cards with the spray adhesive and place the x-ray images on them. Attach each "x-ray" to a can by placing a strip of double-sided sticky tape along one of the short ends on the back of the thick card, then wrapping it around the can with the taped end last.

Sewing Cabinet

YOU WILL NEED:

- a small cabinet with 6 drawers (either painted or plain wood)
- acrylic paint in 7 different colors
- 6 small pebbles
- a black acrylic marker pen (optional)
- pliers
- contact glue

1. Paint the cabinet and drawers in different colors (see photos). **2. Paint** each pebble in the same color as one of the drawers. Leave them to dry. **3. Use** black pen to draw freehand images on each pebble: a button, a needle, scissors, a reel of thread, a thimble, and a tape measure (*see p. 306*). Leave them to dry. **4. Remove** the handles from the drawers (this can be done quite easily using pliers). **5. Mismatch** a painted pebble knob to a different colored drawer, and glue the pebbles in place of the original handles.

English Candy Box

YOU WILL NEED:

- a large pebble
- acrylic paint: bronze, pink, yellow, green, black
- a purple-glazed cardboard box
- glue

1. Paint the pebble bronze and leave it to dry. **2. Paint** English candy shapes on the pebble: square ones, long ones, and round ones. Leave to dry. **3. Glue** the pebble onto the center of the box's lid.

Teddy Box

YOU WILL NEED:

- a clementine box
- sky-blue acrylic paint
- a flat paintbrush
- paper with teddy bear prints
- scissors
- adhesive varnish

1. Paint the clementine box sky-blue inside and out. Leave it to dry and then apply a second coat of paint. Leave it to dry. **2. Carefully** cut out the teddy bear shapes from the paper. **3. Cover** part of the box with adhesive varnish. Place one teddy bear shape on the box and cover it with adhesive varnish. **4. Continue** in this way for the rest of the box, taking care to apply the first coat of adhesive varnish everywhere to avoid differences in shininess. Leave to dry. **5. Apply** a final coat of adhesive varnish over all for evenness.

Office Stationery Set

YOU WILL NEED:

- thin paper with fish, coral, and shell designs
- scissors
- office accessories made from transparent vinyl
- adhesive varnish
- a flat paintbrush

1. Cut out the various designs, leaving a ⅛ of an inch excess around the edges. **2. Choose** where you want to place them and cover just those areas (plus an excess of ⅛ of an inch) with adhesive varnish. Place the cutouts on those chosen spots. Leave to dry. **3. Apply** a second coat of adhesive varnish in the same way, again with an excess of ⅛ of an inch. Leave to dry.

Tea Boxes

YOU WILL NEED:

- tissue paper: pink, orange
- two glass jars with lids
- adhesive varnish
- a flat paintbrush
- paper with printed tea and teapot motifs
- paper with printed green tea leaf motifs
- scissors

1. Cut out different sizes and shapes of triangles from the tissue paper. **2. Cover** part of a jar with adhesive varnish. Place the pieces of tissue paper on top, alternating pink and orange. Apply a thin layer of adhesive varnish on top of the pieces of paper. Cover the whole of the outside of the jars in this way, one area after another. Leave to dry. **3. Carefully** cut out the motifs. Place one cutout and cover it with adhesive varnish. Proceed in this way for both boxes, taking care to apply the first coat of adhesive varnish everywhere to avoid differences in shininess. Leave to dry. **4. Apply** a final coat of adhesive varnish for evenness.

Romance To Go

YOU WILL NEED:

For the model shown (10½ x 8 inches) you will need:

- a cardboard mini-case
- paint primer
- acrylic paint: pink, orange
- a medium-size flat paintbrush
- a very small flat paintbrush
- a large box of golden glitter
- fake leopard fur
- scissors
- double-sided sticky tape
- a sheet of pink paper (8½ x 11)
- a pencil with eraser
- a hole puncher
- a black fine-tipped felt pen

Contents of the mini-case:

- a garter belt
- red and dark-red fabric rose petals
- 2 champagne flutes
- a little music box that plays a love song

1. Apply the primer to the surface (inside and out) of the mini-case. Let it dry. Paint the inside pink and the outside orange (use the smaller brush to paint around the handle and the catch). Apply a second coat of orange paint and sprinkle with glitter before the paint dries. **2. Cut** out a heart from the fake leopard fur, as well as a rectangle that is the same length as the handle and wide enough to wrap around it. Use the double-sided sticky tape to attach the heart to the inside of the lid. Attach the rectangle of fake leopard fur to the handle in the same way. **3. Cut** out little paper hearts and punch holes in them. Write sweet love messages on them and attach them to the clips of the garter belt. Place the rose petals in the bottom of the case, along with the champagne flutes (wrap them in tissue paper if you plan on carrying the case around), the music box, and the garter belt with its hearts.

Seed Saver

YOU WILL NEED:

- transparent plastic (e.g. a shower curtain)
- a ruler
- scissors
- a sheet of flower transfers (preferably to match the flower species of your seeds)
- a flat stick
- clothespins
- aluminum foil
- iron
- flower seeds
- a hole puncher
- fancy eyelets
- eyelet pliers

1. Cut rectangles measuring 5½ x 3¼ inches from the transparent plastic and place a flower transfer in the center of each rectangle. Use the flat stick to rub the transfer until the motif has been entirely transferred onto the plastic. Fold the rectangle in two and use clothespins to keep it folded. Place a piece of aluminum foil on either side of the folded plastic and swiftly iron one of the open sides of the folded square in a straight line so that the two halves of plastic stick together. Do the same for the opposite side, so as to form a little pocket with only the top open. **2. Fill** the pocket with flower seeds (preferably seeds of the same flower depicted in the transfer on the pocket). Close the pocket by making two folds at 90° to those you made to close the sides. Seal the resulting pyramid shape in the same way as before. Punch a hole in the top of the packet and place an eyelet in the hole. Fix it in place with the eyelet pliers.

ILLUSTRATED TECHNIQUES

crochet techniques pp. 53, 88, 137

slip stitch

chain

single crochet

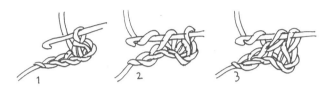

double crochet

embroidery technique pp. 71, 92, 127

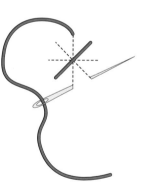

herringbone stitch

star-shaped cross-stitch

French knot

boondoggle techniques pp. 70, 87, 93, 129, 144, 171, 194, 282

FOUR-CORD BOONDOGGLE

Start with a single loop

1. Fold two cords in the middle and form two loops.
2. Use one of the loops to make a knot around the other one.
3. Pull very tight.
4. Start to braid.

Start without single loop

1. Place two cords across the middle of each other crosswise.
2. Hold the intersection firmly.
3. Make the first loop.
4. Make the second loop.
5. Pass one of the ends of the lower cord over the first loop, then through the second.
6. Pass the other end of the lower cord over the second loop, then through the first.
7. Pull the cords tight.
8. Let go and complete the tightening.
9. Start to braid.

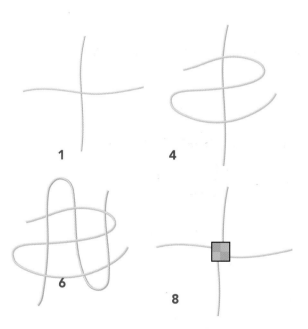

SQUARE BOONDOGGLE

1. Start with or without a loop.
2. Make the first loop.
3. Make the second loop.
4. Pass one of the ends of the lower cord over the first loop, then through the second.
5. Pass the other end of the lower cord over the second loop, then through the first.
6. Pull the stitch tight.
7. Repeat the operation until you have completed the boondoggle.
8. Glue the last stitch and cut off the excess cord.

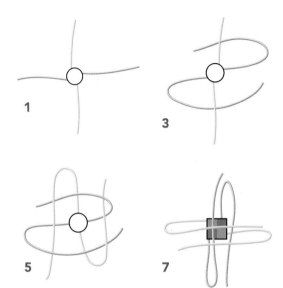

ROUND BOONDOGGLE

1. Start with or without a loop.
2. Make the first loop and position it diagonally.
3. Make the second loop and position it diagonally.
4. Pass one of the ends of the cord that was crossed diagonally over the first loop, then through the second.
5. Pass the other end of the cord that was crossed diagonally over the second loop, then through the first.
6. Pull the stitch tight.
7. Repeat the operation until you have completed the boondoggle.
8. Glue the last stitch and cut off the excess cord.

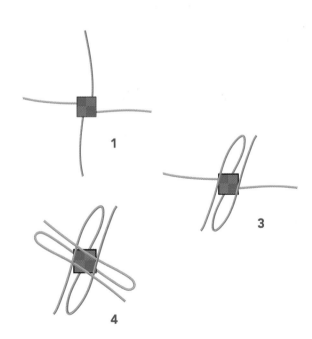

SIX-CORD BOONDOGGLE

1. Make a knot in the middle of a cord around your thumb.

2. Place the middle of two other cords on this knot.

3. Make a second knot to hold these two cords.

4. Place the cords: two on top, two at the bottom, one to the left, and one to the right.

5. Bring the two top cords toward the bottom, slipping one of them between the two bottom cords and placing the other on the side, forming two loops.

6. Bring the side cord to the second loop on the other side, taking it over the two loops.

7. Bring the two bottom cords toward the top in the same way as the first two.

8. Bring the other side cord over and pass it through the first two loops.

9. Pull the stitch tight.

10. Repeat the operation until you have completed the boondoggle.

11. Glue the last stitch and cut off the excess cord.

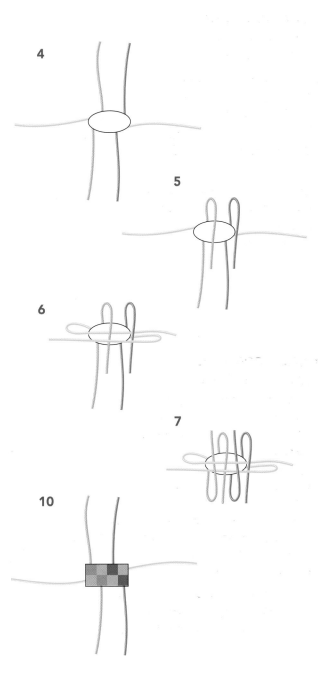

FOUR TO SIX CORDS BOONDOGGLE

1. Place the middle of a cord in the center of the stitch and hold it in place with your finger.

2. Place the cords two at the top, two at the bottom, one to the left, and one to the right.

3. Start to braid the first stitch, as if you were making a six-cord boondoggle, ensuring that you keep the cord you added in place.

4. Bring the two top cords toward the bottom, slipping one of them between the two bottom cords and placing the other on the side, forming two loops.

5. Bring the side cord to the second loop on the other side, taking it over the two loops.

6. Bring the two bottom cords toward the top in the same way as the first two.

7. Bring the other side cord over and pass it through the first two loops.

8. Start to pull the stitch tight and let go of the cord at the last moment.

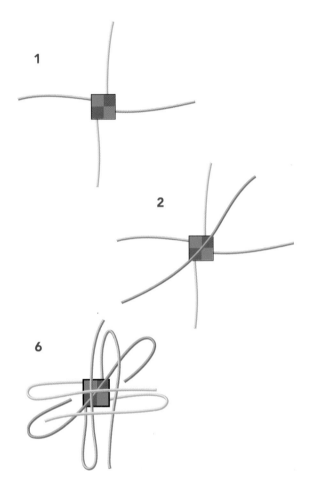

PATTERNS

Checkered Headband p. 104

Felt Flowers p. 103

Flower Barrette
p. 117

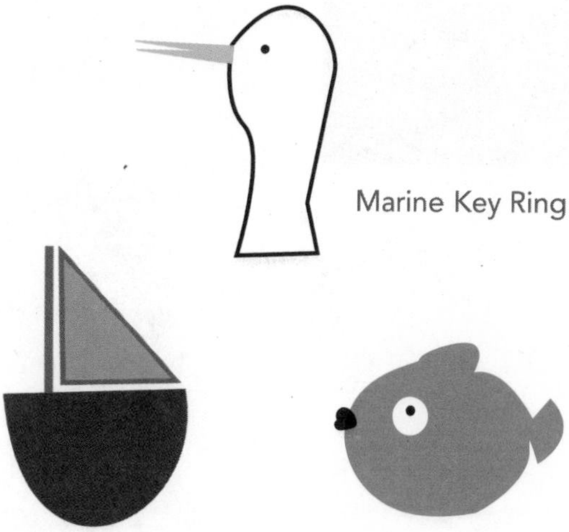

Marine Key Ring p. 105

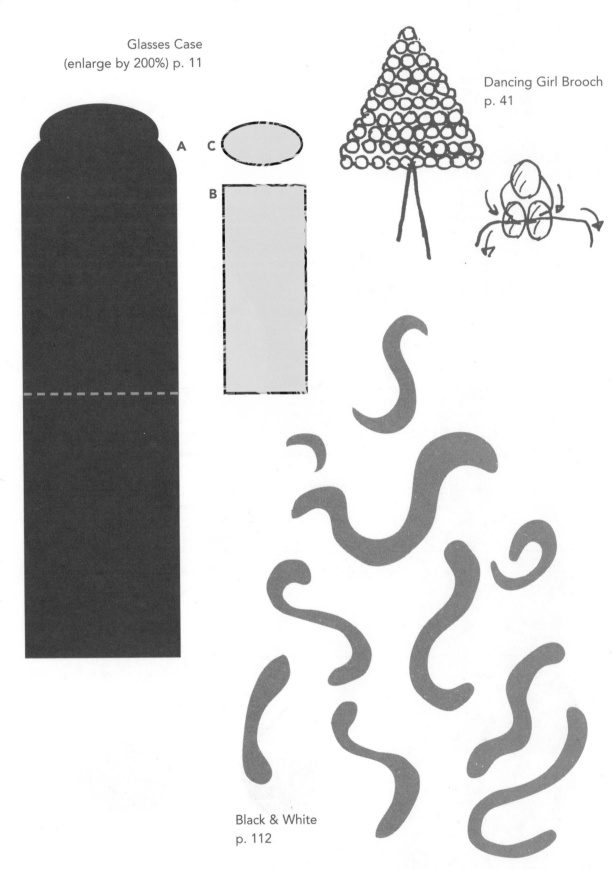

Glasses Case
(enlarge by 200%) p. 11

A   C

B

Dancing Girl Brooch
p. 41

Black & White
p. 112

Flower Ring p. 59

A Purse for Everything p. 16

Flower Carryall p. 18

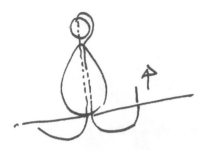

Sea Anemone Ring p. 49

Sun Ring p. 77

Little Beaded Pouch
(enlarge to desired
size) p. 21

Decorated
Paperweights p. 221

petal shape

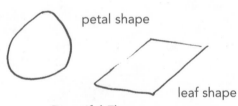

leaf shape

Beautiful Flower
Necklace p. 60

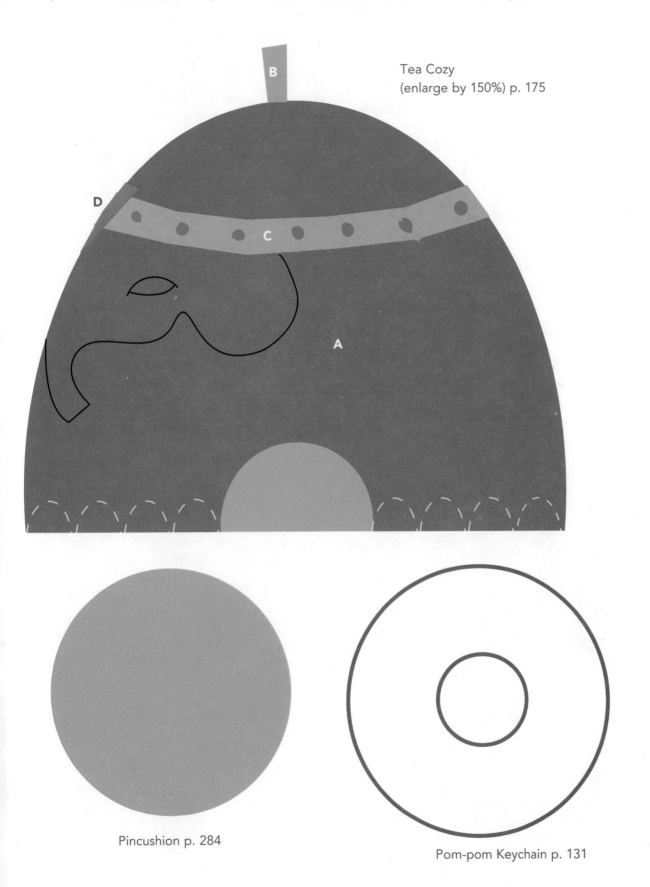

Tea Cozy
(enlarge by 150%) p. 175

B

D

C

A

Pincushion p. 284

Pom-pom Keychain p. 131

Stick a short length of metal wire in each piece.

Add a little clay to finish.

Cut notches for the fingers.

Crown

1. Mold the various pieces:
roll the clay in your hand and shape a large ball for the body. Make a smaller round ball for the head, with a little pointy nose. Shape the arms by making a long thick sausage, then cut it in two. Smooth it out with the tips of your fingers and a little water. To make the crown, flatten a sausage of clay and roll it onto itself at either end, then place it on the end to give it its definitive shape. Cut little notches so as to be able to mold hands and the decoration of the crown. Stick a short length of metal wire in each piece (as in the illustration) and let them dry separately.

2. Joining and gluing:
rub with sandpaper for a better result.

3. Finishing:
Use a little clay to attach the arms and head to the body. Leave to dry.

Roll a sausage of clay on itself.

Sewing Cabinet p. 288

Dragonfly Wrap p. 132

Chopstick Rest p. 168

Best Friend Collage p. 152

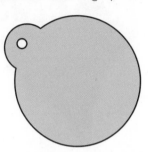

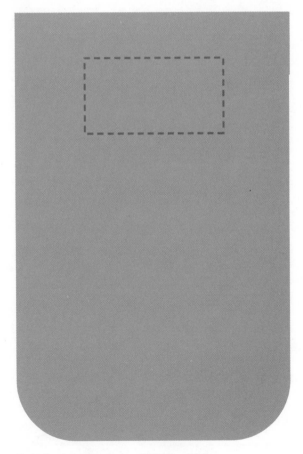

Chessboard p. 203

Felt Bag (enlarge by 300%) p. 20

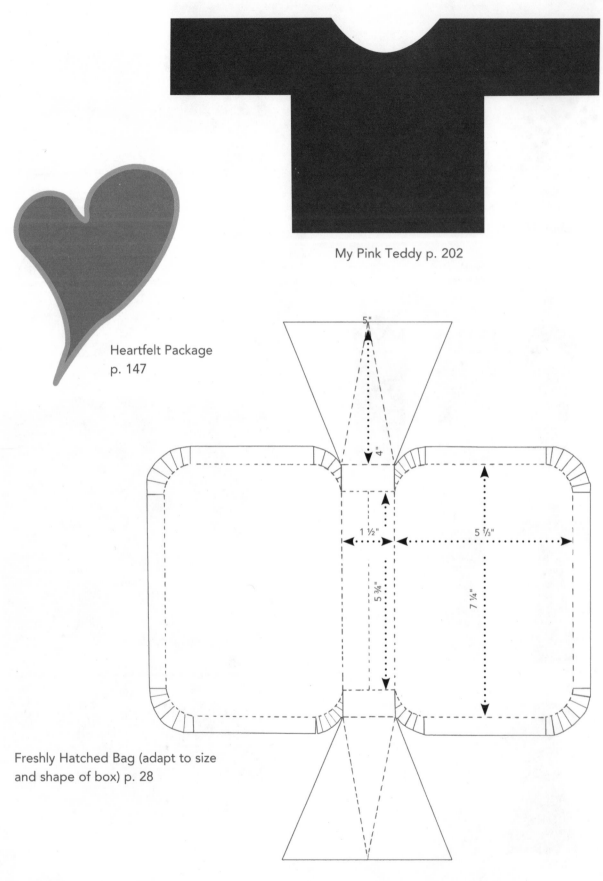

My Pink Teddy p. 202

Heartfelt Package
p. 147

5"

4"

1 ½"

5 ⅓"

5 ¾"

7 ¼"

Freshly Hatched Bag (adapt to size
and shape of box) p. 28

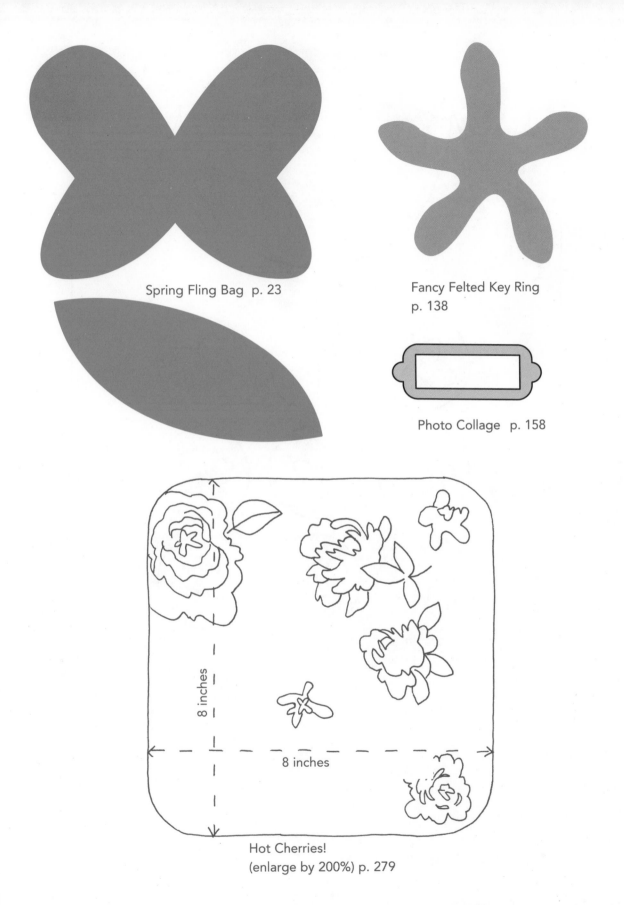

Spring Fling Bag p. 23

Fancy Felted Key Ring
p. 138

Photo Collage p. 158

8 inches

8 inches

Hot Cherries!
(enlarge by 200%) p. 279

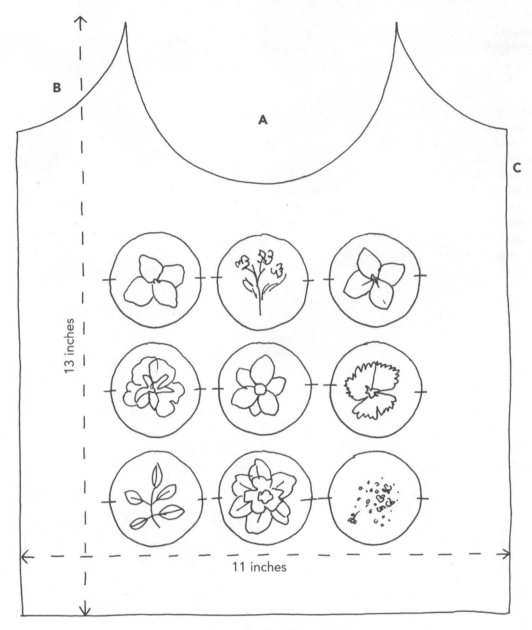

B

A

C

13 inches

11 inches

Spring Flower Bag
(enlarge by 220%) p. 33

INDEX